TOY BOX

Denise Poole

Teacher's book

Oxford University Press

Oxford University Press, Walton Street, Oxford OX2 6DP

Oxford New York Toronto Madrid
Melbourne Auckland
Kuala Lumpur Singapore Hong Kong Tokyo
Delhi Bombay Calcutta Madras Karachi
Nairobi Dar es Salaam Cape Town

and associated companies in
Berlin Ibadan

OXFORD and OXFORD ENGLISH
are trade marks of Oxford University Press

ISBN 0 19 411802 9

Typeset by Oxford University Press

Printed in Hong Kong

Introduction

Toy Box is an audio/oral approach to learning English. It can be used with children from five to nine years of age. The fact that no reading or written work is included in the syllabus means that even children who have not yet begun to read and write in their own language can cope with all the games, songs, rhymes and exercises included in the book.

Reading and writing can be introduced by the teacher if and when appropriate, using simple games like matching words to pictures, copying words, and creating simple sentences from word cards.

Objectives

The objectives of *Toy Box* are:

* to familiarize the children with the verbs *to be* and *to have* and with a selection from the list of the most frequently used words in English, while staying within the confines of the child's world;

* to enable children to ask for and give simple information about themselves and others;

* to develop pronunciation in a natural way;

* to enable children to express simple likes and to talk about abilities.

Last, but by no means least, the objective is to make this first contact with English a thoroughly pleasant and communicative experience.

Vocabulary

Research shows that twelve key words make up one quarter of all the words we read and write. One hundred of them form half, and three hundred about three-quarters of the total number of words found in children's reading. Thus a good working knowledge of these words prepares children effectively for reading and writing. *Toy Box* uses more than one hundred selected words. This vocabulary includes: numbers from one to fifty, colours, fruit, other foods and drinks, animals, shapes, the family, likes, telling the time

(hours only), and some of the most common verbs in daily use.

Components

The materials consist of a Pupil's Activity Book, a Teacher's Book and a class cassette 🔲. Since the Pupil's Book contains no written instructions, the Teacher's Book is essential.

Teaching English to young learners

Teaching young learners requires a very different approach from that used for older age groups. Young children do not possess fully-developed analytical learning skills, and, therefore, they learn best through acquisition. Clearly this cannot be acquisition as in a natural first language environment, where children are constantly exposed to a wide variety of structures and vocabulary. It will be acquisition through a carefully researched and structured syllabus.

Techniques

For the reason outlined above the sentence is used as the basic teaching unit. The sentences are short and simple, but are not analysed in depth.

The techniques used are:

* listening comprehension for colouring and identification

* cut out and stick in illustrations

* cut out dolls

* finger puppets which can be used as a substitute for physical movement where the environment does not offer sufficient space

* cut out cards to be used as flash cards for identifying objects and to be used in the guessing games

* songs and rhymes for consolidation and intonation

* games for consolidation through play.

An average child's concentration span is ten to fifteen minutes, so the activities have been designed for this.

No activity should last longer, unless the teacher can see that the children are still totally absorbed in what they are doing. If the children begin to show signs of boredom, the teacher should not hesitate to change the activity. It can always be returned to later if the content has not been assimilated.

Materials necessary

The children will need a classroom set of safety scissors and glue. If they do not possess their own personal sets of coloured pencils, felt tips or crayons, these will be necessary too. Coloured card for mounting flashcards will also prove useful.

The characters

The clown characters were chosen because they are fundamentally timeless and placeless. Circuses and clowns appear in most cultures and are particularly appealing to children. They are happy, colourful, characters who can be easily identified by very young children.

Coco is a clown, but he is also a child. Like our pupils he has his family, his mother, father, sister and brother. He is an exotic figure but he also has a great deal in common with the children we are teaching.

What interests children today

A survey carried out in Great Britain a few years ago, with the aim of establishing exactly what interests young children today, gave the following results:

toys	comics	animals	space
music	war games	food/sweets	TV/video
football (for boys)			

Toy Box does not cover all the topics listed, but it includes all the more traditional interests, while remaining within the range of the most widely used vocabulary in English. It also features two of the characters which appear in the best-known fairy stories, a witch and a princess.

Stimulation

Almost every child wishes to be the centre of attention in one way or another, and is willing to give his/her best to be just that. It is this spirit of competition that should be exploited to the full. While prize giving can be negative and create unhealthy jealousy, group competition can be quite the opposite. A satisfactory way of organizing this can be a point chart.

For a point chart, the children are divided into mixed ability groups (i.e. with strong and weak pupils in every group). These groups can be identified by colours. A chart can then be made (see below).

The activities and games can contribute to a points system, the group with the highest score being awarded a point at the end of an activity or game.

	week 1	week 2	week 3	week 4
the red group				
the green group				
the blue group				
the pink group				
the yellow group				
the orange group				
the purple group				

Where writing has not been introduced, blocks of the appropriate colour can be used. The children can also wear badges with their group colour to facilitate identification. For this first chart, colour has been suggested, because the vocabulary is to be found in the very first pages of the book, but later other categories such as fruit or animals can be used.

Total physical response

The expression 'total physical response' (TPR) means that the children physically carry out the movements or gestures of the activity. There are two reasons for TPR exercises: the first is that assimilation is through association, and, as a consequence is more thorough and rapid; the second is that children who are not used to remaining seated for long periods of time, are given the chance to move. The action rhymes are designed for this.

How each section works

Each phase of each lesson is designed to last from five to fifteen minutes, so as to coincide with the pupils' concentration span. In some cases the phase is divided into stages, i.e. teacher presentation and participation – class answering – group answering – individual answering – role play – pair work. Most school syllabuses programme two or three hours of English lessons weekly. Any differences in time available can be catered for by spending more or less time on the games, songs and rhymes. The children may have a game which they want to repeat if time permits.

Listening to the cassette is the first phase of many sections and the use of the cassette is often necessary for correct pronunciation.

In most listening activities the 'pause' button should be used so that the children have time to do the activity without rushing and becoming confused. The symbol [P] is used in the transcripts to indicate where a pause is appropriate. The length of the pause should be gauged according to the speed of an average pupil. In colour dictation, once the colour key has been established, slower pupils can complete their colouring later.

The symbols

Six symbols are used in *Toy Box.* Each one represents an activity type.

Listening

Speaking

Drawing

Colouring

Singing

Cutting out and sticking

Presenting the lesson

When introducing new vocabulary or structures remember that children need to be given a great deal of confidence, so material should be presented slowly and thoroughly.

Let's look at the presentation of the first lesson. Start by introducing yourself to the children. *Hello! I'm . . .* After greeting the children in this way and pointing to yourself several times, point to one of the children and say *Hello!* Encourage the child to reply in the same way. Then repeat *Hello!* and add *I'm (your name).* The child can then say *Hello!* and (pointing to him/herself) add *I'm (his/her name).* If necessary prompt with the child's name in order to be sure that the meaning of the question and answer has been understood. If you are using the cassette then make appropriate gestures, i.e. for *Hello!* walk towards one of the children and imitate expressions and gestures which are used in real life when meeting another person. For *I'm . . .* point to yourself and when the reply is given on the cassette, point to the child in question.

Greet other children in the same way and get them to answer. When you are satisfied that this mini-dialogue has been understood, the children can begin to repeat it among themselves and you can move around the class helping and making suggestions where necessary. Always praise and encourage the children with *Good*, *Very good*, or *Well done*.

Dialogues

Dialogues should be broken down into sections, practised and then put together in their complete form.

This is the first complete dialogue:

> *Hello!*
>
> *Hello! I'm (Peter). What's your name?*
>
> *(Mary.) I'm (Mary).*

You have already covered the first phase *Hello! Hello! I'm (Mary)* of the dialogue as an introduction so now continue with the second phase.

> *I'm (Peter). What's your name?*
>
> *(Mary.) I'm (Mary).*

Practise first in chorus with the entire class asking *What's your name?* then move on to groups and finally individuals. When working with individuals choose the faster, stronger pupils first. This will enable the slower, weaker pupils to hear the dialogue more often before being called on to perform.

Classroom vocabulary

Throughout *Toy Box* you will need to use a number of expressions in English to encourage or direct pupils. The list over the page will be found the most useful.

Bring me	Look	Stand up
Colour	Look at the picture	Take your book
Come here	Open your book	Thank you
Cut	please	That's right
Draw	Quiet please	Turn around
Glue	scissors	Very good
Good	Show me	Well done
Hold up	Sing	What's her name?
Listen	Sit down	What's his name?

Vocabulary – identifying things

The second part of the lesson teaches the numbers one to five. Begin by listening to the tape. Write the numbers on the board or use fingers or flash cards. Begin by saying *one*. Let the children repeat and then add *two*. The children can repeat *one, two*. Hold up the card for number three and say *three*. The children can repeat *three*. Now hold up the cards for one, two and three and invite the children to say the numbers as they are shown. Continue in the same way for four and five. When you are satisfied that the numbers have been learned, hold up the number cards out of sequence. Let the children say the numbers all together, then in groups and finally as individuals.

Teach the five colours in the same way. The children can then listen to the tape and colour the numbers. The number cards can be cut out and the game 'Bring Me' can be played.

Correcting

Do not interrupt a child who is speaking. Remember he or she is making a great effort to assimilate and reproduce new words and structures as well as sounds which may be very different from those in his or her own language.

Interruption can cause a psychological block. Perhaps the most satisfactory way of dealing with mistakes is to simply repeat the sentence correctly when the child has finished speaking. When there is hesitation in replying, prompt quietly with the correct answer. Never highlight mistakes unless they are general mistakes and then direct corrections to the class, not an individual. When the sentence has been heard a number of times the correction should become automatic. Some corrections can be made later when the pupils are more relaxed and you are certain that no damage will be done.

The importance of games

Games are of fundamental importance in the primary language class. They incorporate all the vital factors necessary for teaching young learners:

- the child as a protagonist
- movement
- repetition and consolidation without boredom
- encouragement of emulation
- participation in group activities
- reflection of a child's fantasy world

The games in this book have also been specifically designed or chosen to reflect the structure and vocabulary being learnt. Their descriptions can be found on pages 7–8.

Songs and rhymes for listening and oral assimilation

Songs and rhymes are also important for young learners. They are often one of the most popular parts of the lesson, while providing models of correct rhythm, pronunciation and intonation.

The songs and rhymes in *Toy Box* are carefully graded so that the children begin with the easiest and gradually move on to more difficult ones. If the songs or rhymes are quite long, begin by teaching the first verse or part only. The rest can be taught later. If you can find other songs or rhymes related to the lesson content, so much the better. In *Toy Box* all the songs and rhymes have been designed to repeat the content of the various phases of the lessons, with as few new words as possible. The words of the songs and rhymes are to be found on the appropriate pages of this guide.

Teaching aids

A variety of equipment is available to the teacher in the classroom.

- The **blackboard** can be used for quick sketches. It is not necessary to be a good artist; what is important is that the children can interpret the illustrations. Simplified illustrations like matchstick men are fine. Very often children will appreciate the humour of a rapid line drawing more than a sophisticated work of art. If a whiteboard is available it is preferable to a blackboard. With coloured pens drawings can be produced which are more attractive and easier to remember.

- The **felt board** gives greater flexibility than the blackboard but figures have to be pre-prepared. Sometimes they can be bought or the collaboration of the school art teacher can be sought. Figures should be as colourful and interesting as possible.

- **Audio cassettes** have already been discussed. Remember to find the correct place on the cassette before the lesson to avoid time-wasting and confusion.

- **Posters** can be easily made and the same poster can be used in many different situations. Excellent posters for fruit and flowers can be made from gardening catalogues and weekly or monthly magazines can be used for clothing. Other excellent posters can be purchased.

- An **overhead projector** (OHP) can be used with pre-prepared or spot drawings. These can then be kept and used at a later date.

Picture Dictionary

The Picture Dictionary (pages 37–42) is an optional activity which can be used with pupils who have already some writing ability. It can be exploited in two ways. Firstly, the pupils should simply draw a line linking the picture with the appropriate word(s). Secondly, they can write the word(s) under or next to the appropriate picture.

The Games

Squeak Piggy Squeak

The children sit in a circle with one blindfolded child in the middle. The child in the centre is turned around several times so their sense of direction is lost and it becomes impossible for them to remember who is sitting where. Then the blindfolded child moves around the circle and sits on the lap of one of the children and says: *Squeak, piggy, squeak!* The child whose lap is

being sat upon then squeaks like a pig. The blindfolded child must try to guess the name of the other child, and asks questions like *Are you (Mary)?* receiving the answer, *Yes, I am* or *No, I'm not*. The game continues until the name is correctly guessed. Then the child whose name has been guessed is blindfolded and the game begins again. If preferred, music can be played and the child must stop and sit on the lap of the nearest child every time the music stops. This game can become very noisy. To play a quieter version the blindfolded child stands in front of the class with their back towards the class. The teacher then points to another child who comes forward and touches the first. Then the blindfolded child says *Squeak, piggy, squeak!* and the game continues as before.

Later when the children know the names of other animals the game can be adapted to use these words:

> *Hiss snake, hiss!*
>
> *Roar lion, roar!*
>
> *Screech parrot, screech!*
>
> *Sing bird, sing!*
>
> *Chatter monkey, chatter!*

The Number Guessing Game

The children play this game within their own groups or as opposing groups. Each child is given a card with a number on it and the other children take it in turns to try and guess the number. *Is it number three? Yes, it is*, or *No, it isn't*. The child who guesses a number correctly is given a point and the child (or group) with the highest number of points is the winner.

The Colour Guessing Game

This is played in the same way as the number guessing game but colour cards are used instead of number cards.

The Object Guessing Game

For this a series of flash cards representing categories of vocabulary (animals, fruit or food) are used, and the game is played as for the other guessing games. If animals are being used the question can be *Are you a (monkey)? Yes, I am*, or *No, I'm not*. If other vocabulary is used then the question should be *Is it (an orange)? Yes, it is*, or *No it isn't*. Award points as in the other games.

Simon Says

Here a leader stands in front of the class and gives commands which are either of the type *Simon says – stand up!* or, simply, *Stand up!* If the command is preceded by *Simon says* then all the other children obey. If the leader does not say *Simon says* then the children must not move. Any child who moves is eliminated. The game is played until only one child remains. He or she is then the winner and becomes the next leader. A point can be awarded to the winner's group.

One Potato –Two Potatoes

The children play this in pairs. The first child holds out his hand palm downwards and says: *One potato!* The second child then puts his hand on top of the other child's hand and says: *Two potatoes!* The first child puts his other hand on top and says: *Three potatoes!* the second child puts his hand on top and says *Four!* The first child pulls his first hand out from underneath the other hands and puts it on top and says: *Five potatoes!* The game continues until the rhyme has been completed. The objective is to get faster and faster as the game proceeds.

The complete words are as follows:

> *One potato!*
>
> *Two potatoes!*
>
> *Three potatoes!*
>
> *Four!*
>
> *Five potatoes!*
>
> *Six potatoes!*
>
> *Seven potatoes!*
>
> *More!*

This game usually involves a great deal of hilarity and hand slapping!

What's in the Bag?

The materials necessary for this game are a bag (which must not be transparent) and real objects, plastic models or flash cards representing the objects in question. The teacher first shows a selection of objects but puts only some of them into the bag. The children must not see which ones are included and which are excluded. Then they take turns to ask, *Is there (a banana) in the bag? Yes, there is. No, there isn't.* For every correct guess a point is awarded.

This game can be played in groups or between opposing groups.

Bring Me

1 Numbers

For this game the children are divided into groups. There will usually be five children in each group, but the number may vary according to the number of words to be practised. Each of the five children is given a card with one of the numbers from one to five written on it. The teacher calls out *Number two!* All the children holding number two cards then run to the teacher. The first to arrive is given a point for his/her group.

2 Colours

This is played as above but the children are given colour cards, and the command is *Bring me (red)!*

3 Numbers and colours

For this game each child in a group is given a number and the whole group is given colour cards which should be put in the middle in such a way as to be easily accessible to all. The teacher now calls out *Number threes – bring me red!* All the children who have the 'three' cards then pick up the red colour card and run to the teacher. Again the first to arrive is awarded a point for their team.

Should this game cause too much excitement then holding up the card can be substituted for the running.

Objects, foods, fruits, animals and adjectives can also be used as the children progress through the book.

The Animal Game

Each child in a group is given a card representing an animal, which is not shown to the other children. Then the other members of the group (or an opposing group) ask questions in turn: *Are you an elephant? No, I'm not. Are you a seal? No, I'm not. Are you a penguin? Yes, I am.* If you wish, when the children reply in the affirmative, they can imitate the animal they are pretending to be. This same game can also be played with fruit or other categories of vocabulary.

Wordlist

The vocabulary used in *Toy Box*, and the page on which each item first appears, are listed below. The numbers *one* to *fifty* are also taught in *Toy Box*.

address	29
and	4
apple	9
arm	28
ball	11
balloon	2
banana	9
beautiful	26
behind	27
bicycle	15
big	16
bird	7
birthday	9
biscuits	8
black	3
blackboard	12
blonde	26
blue	1
boat	16
book	3
box	15
bread	31
brother	5
brown	3
cake	8
Can I help you?	31
Can you see ...?	25
candle	9
car	2
carrot	31
cat	7
chair	12
cherries	31

chocolate	8
circle	21
clock	30
close	17
clown	26
coffee	8
cold	33
cook	35
corner	19
cornflakes	31
crocodile	25
dance	35
desk	3
Do you like?	8
dog	5
doll	16
door	12
draw	34
dress	22
drum	16
ear	28
egg	31
elephant	25
fat	26
father	5
fish	31
flagpole	25
floor	19
fly	35
foot	28
fork	31
giraffe	25
gloves	23
go	2
Good morning	31
grapes	31
green	1
grey	6
hand	28
happy	32
Has he/she got ...?	15

hat	9
Have they got ...?	20
Have you got ...?	16
He's	9
He's got	15
heart	21
Hello	cover
her	4
his	4
honey	31
hot	33
house	2
How are you?	14
How many ... are there?	9
How old are you?	9
hungry	33
I	cover
I like	8
I'm	cover
I'm fine, thanks	14
ice-cream	8
in	19
in front of	27
Is there a ... ?	7
it's	1
jeans	22
jump	6
kangaroo	24
kite	15
knife	31
lamb	7
leg	28
lemon	10
like	10
lion	25
milk	10
monkey	25
mother	5
mouth	28
mushrooms	31
my	5

near	19	She's	9	ugly	26
neck	28	She's got	15	under	20
new	26	shirt	22		
No	1	shoes	22	wait	2
No, I don't	10	short	16	walk	6
No, I haven't	16	sing	34	want	31
No, it isn't	9	sister	5	What are they?	2
No, there isn't	7	skirt	22	What colour?	1
No, they haven't	20	small	16	What is it?	2
nose	9	snake	25	What's missing?	36
number	1	socks	22	What's the time?	30
		spoon	31	What's your name?	cover
o'clock	30	square	21	where	19
old	26	star	21	whistle	15
on	19	stop	2	white	4
or	16	strawberries	8	Who is it?	5
orange	1	stretch	8	window	12
orangeade	10	sun	2	witch	26
		sweater	23		
paint	3	sweets	8	yellow	1
parrot	7	swim	35	Yes	1
pear	9			Yes, I have	16
peas	31	T-shirt	22	Yes, it is	9
pen	3	table	12	Yes, there is	7
pencil	3	tall	16	Yes, they have	20
penguin	24	tea	8	young	33
pink	2	teddy bear	15		
play	34	telephone	13	zoo	24
please	31	tell	35		
poor	32	tennis	34		
princess	26	tent	25		
puppet	16	thank you	31		
purple	2	There are	9		
		thin	26		
read	34	thirsty	33		
rectangle	21	This is	5		
red	1	tiger	24		
rich	32	tired	32		
ride	34	toes	9		
run	17	tomato	31		
		touch	9		
sad	32	traffic-lights	2		
sausages	31	train	16		
scarf	23	triangle	21		
seal	24	trousers	23		
shape	21	trumpet	9		

Cover

Active vocabulary
Hello   I'm   What's your name?

Play the song 'Toy Box'. The pupils should listen several times and sing along if they can, but it is not necessary to teach the song.

> Here is the toy box
> Full of toys.
> All good things
> For girls and boys.
>
> A drum, a trumpet,
> A teddy bear.
> A train and a boat,
> And the doll is there.
>
> Here is the toy box
> Full of toys.
> All good things
> For girls and boys.

1   Greet the pupils with *Hello, boys and girls*. As you say *boys* indicate a number of boys in the class. Indicate some girls as you say *girls*. Do this several times. Invite the pupils to reply together and then individually with *Hello*. Say your name *I'm …* Repeat this several times, pointing to yourself. If possible, explain that this is how you will greet each other at the beginning of each lesson. Ask the pupils questions individually. Choose one pupil and ask *What's your name?* Help him or her to answer with his or her own name – for example *David* or *I'm David*. Encourage pupils by saying *Good!* or *Very good!* Ask the pupils to look at the cover of *Toy Box* and play the cassette. Point out Coco and Candy to them as they listen.

> Hello! I'm Coco. What's your name?
> Candy! I'm Candy. What's your name?
> Mandy! I'm Mandy. What's your name?
> David! I'm David. What's your name?
> What's your name? [P]   What's your name? [P]

The pupils should listen two or probably three times. Then play (or say yourself) *What's your name?* and get the whole class to repeat it. Then move on to repetition in groups and finally with individuals.

2   When the expression *What's your name?* has been assimilated by the class, divide the pupils into pairs or groups. Each pair or group should practise this dialogue, substituting their own names. Show them how to do this by choosing one group first to demonstrate. The dialogue should run like this:

Pupil 1   *Hello. I'm Mary. What's your name?*
Pupil 2   *David. I'm David. What's your name?*
Pupil 3   *Kim. I'm Kim. What's your name?* etc.

Page 1   part 1

Active vocabulary
yes   no   Squeak piggy squeak

1   The pupils open their books at page C5 and cut out the picture of Coco. This should be glued over the picture of Coco on page 1. Instructions for this should be given in English as far as possible – showing the pupils at the same time what you want them to do. A considerable amount of repetition will be necessary, but it is useful for pupils to become accustomed to instructions in English. Don't hesitate, however, to use the pupils' own language if they are having difficulty in understanding. Say *Open your books at page C5, please* (show the page). *Take your scissors* (do this yourself). *Cut out the picture of Coco* (cut it out yourself – or mime it). *Now open your books at page 1. Glue the picture here.* The pupils should then draw a picture of themselves in the larger frame on the right of page 1. Say *Draw a picture of yourself. Draw it here, please.* When the picture is finished, divide the pupils into groups. Beginning with one group as an example, get the pupils to point to the picture of themselves and say *I'm (Mary)*. Get them to say in addition *What's your name?* and wait for the answer. Then within each group get pupils to do the same.

2   With a more confident class, and if time permits, play 'Squeak, piggy, squeak!' See page 7 for instructions.

3   Play the song 'What's your name?'

> What's your name? What's your name?
> I'm Francesca. I'm Francesca.
> What's your name? What's your name?
> I'm Juan Carlos. I'm Juan Carlos.
> What's your name? What's your name?
> I'm Christian. I'm Christian.
> What's your name? What's your name?
> I'm Dominique. I'm Dominique.

The pupils sing along with the cassette several times until they have learnt it. Then they should insert their own names. One pupil starts, and when he or she has sung *What's your name?* indicate another pupil to answer, and so continue the song. The song will thus 'chain' around the classroom.

Page 1 part 2

Active vocabulary

one two three four five yellow green red blue orange it's What colour's this? What number's this?

1   Play the numbers one to five.

    One [P], two [P], three [P], four [P], five. [P]

There are a number of ways in which numbers can be taught. As you say the numbers (or as you play the cassette) you can hold up the appropriate number of fingers. Alternatively, the figures can be written on a blackboard or on cards to be held up. First teach the numbers in sequence and get the pupils to repeat them. Once they have been mastered, indicate numbers out of sequence. Ask the pupils to say the number in English. This should be done first with the whole class, then with individual pupils.

2   The pupils cut out the number cards for numbers one to five from page C5. For extra strength the pupils should stick the numbers to pieces of card of the appropriate size. If different coloured card is used ensure that each number is stuck to a different colour and that all the pupils are using the same colour for the same number (e.g. all number twos should be red, number threes blue etc.). Only the five colours taught on this page (yellow, red, green, blue and orange) should be used.

3   Play the song 'Numbers'.

    One, two, three, four, five.
    One, two, three, four, five.
    One, two, three, four, five.
    One, two, three, four, five.

    Five, four, three, two, one.
    Five, four, three, two, one.
    Five, four, three, two, one.
    Five, four, three, two, one.

Let the pupils listen and then sing along with the cassette.

4   Play the team game 'Bring me' (page 8), using numbers one to five.

5   Play the sentences. Hold up the appropriate colour as it is said. Pause after each colour and give the pupils the opportunity of repeating *It's yellow*, *It's red*, and assimilating the colours.

    Look! It's yellow. [P]
    Look! It's red. [P]
    Look! It's green. [P]
    Look! It's blue. [P]
    Look! It's orange. [P]

Then, using colour cards or objects, ask the pupils the question *What colour's this?* Do this first with the whole class and then with individual pupils. If the class is confident, get some of the pupils to ask the question instead of you. If they find the question too difficult, one pupil can simply hold up a card silently and invite another to say what colour it is. When both question and answers are well assimilated, divide the pupils into groups or pairs to continue practising. If the pupils have stuck their numbers to coloured cards these can be used. If white card has been used then the back of each number card should be coloured. The pupils can work in groups or pairs, asking and answering, holding up cards silently or saying *What colour's this?*

6   Play the colour dictation.

    Number five – colour it green. [P]
    Number three – colour it blue. [P]
    Number four – colour it red. [P]
    Number two – colour it orange. [P]
    Number one – colour it yellow. [P]

The pupils listen to the cassette and colour the numbers in their books. You may have to show them what to do at first. Pause the cassette after each sentence to allow the pupils to colour before moving on to the next sentence. Play the cassette again so they can check their work. Some pupils may be very slow colourers. As long as they have got some of the correct colour onto each number they can finish their colouring later.

7   Teach the commands *Stand up* and *Sit down*. Do this by standing up and sitting down yourself and saying the words. Then mime for the pupils to do the same. Play the game 'Simon Says' using *stand up* and *sit down* (see page 8 for instructions).

8   Play the game 'Guessing' using number cards (see page 7 for instructions).

9   Play the game 'Guessing' using colour cards (see page 7 for instructions).

Page 2

Active vocabulary

purple pink house sun traffic-lights balloon car stop wait go What is it? What are they?

1 Warm up by practising the questions *What's your name? What number's this? What colour's this?* from the previous lesson.

2 Play the cassette to revise the colours already taught (red, green, blue, yellow and orange) and introduce the new colours (purple and pink). As the colours are spoken on the cassette hold up the appropriate colour card or object. Pause after each object to allow the pupils to repeat.

> Look! It's red. [P]
> Look! It's pink. [P]
> Look! It's blue. [P]
> Look! It's green. [P]
> Look! It's purple. [P]
> Look! It's orange. [P]

3 Teach *balloon, house, sun, car,* and *traffic-lights.* Do this by playing the cassette and letting the pupils identify the objects by their numbers. Get the pupils to repeat *It's a car, It's a balloon* and so on. Don't worry about *traffic-lights* being in the plural. The pupils will probably not worry about the difference between singular and plural here.

> Look at number two! It's a car. [P]
> Look at number three! It's a balloon. [P]
> Look at number one! They're traffic-lights. [P]
> Look at number four! It's a house. [P]
> Look at number five! It's the sun. [P]

Consolidate if possible by holding up or pointing to pictures of the objects and getting the pupils to repeat as a class. Ask the questions *What is it?* or *What are they?* as you do this so that they can begin to assimilate them. They can then work in pairs or groups, one pointing to objects and if possible asking *What is it?* and the other answering. Don't worry at this stage if pupils are using the singular form with *traffic-lights* or *a* with *sun.* The pupils should cut out the illustrations from page C5 and stick them over the appropriate pictures on page 2.

4 Colour dictation. Play the cassette, pausing after each colour to enable the pupils to colour the appropriate balloon.

> Look at balloon number four! [P] Colour it purple. [P]
> Look at balloon number five! [P] Colour it red. [P]
> Look at balloon number three! [P] Colour it pink. [P]
> Look at balloon number one! [P] Colour it blue. [P]
> Look at balloon number two! [P] Colour it yellow. [P]

5 Play the rhyme 'Traffic-lights'. The pupils should point to the colours as they join in the rhyme. You may feel the pupils need a translation of this rhyme in order to understand it

> The traffic lights are red, orange, green.
> At red we stop, stop, stop.
> At orange we wait, wait, wait.
> At green we go, go, go.

6 Repeat the songs 'Numbers' and 'What's your name?'

7 Play the game 'Guessing' using colours, including the new ones (purple and pink).

8 If you are using the picture dictionary, pupils should turn to page 37 and write in the new vocabulary (*traffic-lights, sun, car, balloon*).

Page 3

Active vocabulary

pen pencil book paint desk black brown

1 Warm up by practising the questions *What's this? What number's this? What colour's this?* from the previous lessons.

2 Numbers dictation. Play the cassette. The pupils will need some help in understanding what to do. You can do this by doing the first with them on the board, pointing out how to join up the numbers. These have to be joined in the order given on the cassette in order to finish the picture correctly. The dots are **not** joined in numerical order. If necessary explain in the pupils' own language, but demonstration will probably be more effective.

> Look at number one [P]. Three [P] - two [P] - five [P] - one [P] - four [P].
> Look at number three [P]. Two [P] - one [P] - five [P] - three [P] - four [P].
> Look at number four [P]. Three [P] - five [P] - two [P] - four [P] - one [P].
> Look at number two [P]. Three [P] - one [P] - four [P] - two [P] - five [P].
> Look at number five [P]. One [P] - five [P] - three [P] - two [P] - four [P].

The pupils listen and join the dots in each picture in the order on the cassette. Pause the cassette so as to give pupils the opportunity of joining the dots, and check their work after completing each picture.

3   Play the cassette and use cards or objects in the classroom to teach the vocabulary.

> ☺ Look at number one.[P] It's a book. [P]
> Look at number four.[P] It's a desk. [P]
> Look at number two.[P] It's a pen.[P]
> Look at number five.[P] It's a pencil. [P]
> Look at number three.[P] It's paint. [P]

Pupils should repeat *It's a pen* etc. after the cassette. Then practise asking and answering questions like *What's this? It's a pencil*, first with the whole class, then in groups or pairs.

4   Teach *black* and *brown*, using cards or objects, as in the previous lesson. Using cards or objects revise the other colours already learnt (*red*, *blue*, *green*, *yellow*, *orange*, *pink*, *purple*).

5   Colour dictation. Play the cassette giving the pupils sufficient time to colour each picture.

> ☹ Look at the desk![P] It's brown. [P]
> Look at the pen! [P]It's blue. [P]
> Look at the pencil![P] It's orange. [P]
> Look at the book![P] It's green. [P]
> Look at the paint! [P]It's purple. [P]

When they have finished, or have made considerable progress on their colouring (which they can finish later, if necessary), play the next section of the cassette, pausing at the end of each object for the pupils to repeat *It's a green book* etc.

> ☺ Look at number one! [P]It's a green book. [P]
> Look at number two! [P] It's a blue pen. [P]
> Look at number three! [P] It's purple paint. [P]
> Look at number four! [P] It's a brown desk. [P]
> Look at number five! [P] It's an orange pencil. [P]

6   Play the game 'Simon says' (see page 8). Use the instructions *Bring me a* (pencil, pen, book, number one, number two etc.) *Show me a* (pencil, pen, book, number one, number two etc.), *Stand up! Sit down!* You will have to teach *Bring me* and *Show me* if the pupils have not already encountered these passively. Do this by miming, and if necessary explaining in their own language. Begin by giving the orders yourself, then choose one or two of the more able pupils to do so. If you feel the class can manage, this can be played in groups.

7   Repeat the 'Traffic lights' rhyme.

8   Play the game 'Guessing' (see page 7 for instructions). Use cards with sun, house, traffic-lights, balloon, car, pencil, pen, desk, book, and paint.

9   If you are using the picture dictionary, pupils should turn to page 37 and write in the vocabulary (*house*, *book*, *desk*, *pen*, *pencil*, *paint*).

Page 4

Active vocabulary
his   her   and   white

1   Warm up with questions and vocabulary from pages 1, 2 and 3.

2   Ask one of the girls *What's your name?* Wait for her answer and then point at her, and ask the question *What's her name?* The other pupils may be able to answer, at this stage giving simply her name. They may need a little encouragement at first. Then do the same with several more girls. Then do the same with boys, asking *What's his name?*

3   Now try and get the pupils to answer with a phrase *His name's Paul* or *Her name's Katy*. You will have to ask and answer the question with both boys and girls before the pupils fully understand and can repeat.

4   Invite the pupils to ask and answer questions about one another, either as a whole class or in smaller groups.

5   Before doing this colour dictation, the pupils should cut out the pictures of Coco and Candy from page C6 and stick them in their books.

> ☺ Look at Coco!
> Look at his balloon! It's red. [P]
> Look at his book! It's blue. [P]
> Look at his car! It's yellow. [P]
> Look at his house! It's red and white. [P]
> Look at his pen! It's black and yellow. [P]
>
> Look at Candy!
> Look at her balloon! It's pink. [P]
> Look at her car! It's green. [P]
> Look at her desk! It's red. [P]
> Look at her pen! It's blue and yellow.[P]
> Look at her book! It's orange. [P]

6 When the pupils have finished colouring, play the next section of the cassette. The pupils listen to the questions and answer them. Pause the cassette if necessary to give them time to answer. They should answer together as a class.

> 😐 What colour's his book?[P]
> What colour's her pen?[P]

Continue, asking the following questions to the class *What colour's his car? What colour's his house? What colour's his pen? What colour's his desk? What colour's his balloon? What colour's her book?* Use *his* and *her* rather than the names Coco and Candy. If the class are answering well, they could continue in pairs, asking and answering the same type of questions.

7 Get the pupils to cut out the action pictures from page C6 and stick them at the bottom of the page.

8 Play the action rhyme 'Stand up and turn around'.

> 😐 One, stand up. Two, turn around. Three, sit down. Stand up, turn around, sit down.

The pupils do the actions and join in the rhyme. Play the rhyme several times. They can also say the rhyme and act it out without the cassette.

Page 5 part 1

Active vocabulary
my brother sister father mother Who is it? This is … dog

1 Play the cassette. Coco introduces his family. The pupils listen and then repeat the last two words of each section.

> 😐 Hello, I'm Coco.
> Look at number one! This is my sister. [P]
> Look at number two! This is my brother. [P]
> Look at number three! This is my father. [P]
> Look at number four! This is my mother. [P]

Ensure that pupils have understood *my*. Use mime, holding up objects, contrasting, for example, *my pen* with *his pen* or *her pen*.

2 When you feel they have assimilated the vocabulary, ask them questions like these *Number one. Who is it? Number two. Who is it?* Accept the answer *father* or *mother* but encourage pupils to use fuller answers *it's his father* or *it's his mother*.

3 Get the pupils to continue the practise working in pairs or groups.

4 Ask the pupils to colour the pictures of Coco and his family at the top of the page.

Page 5 part 2

1 Ask the pupils to colour the picture of the clown family at the bottom of the page.

2 Play the cassette.

> 😐 Hello, I'm Coco.
> This is me and my family.
> This is my father, my mother, my sister and my brother.
> This is my dog. (*Dog barks*)

3 Ensure that pupils have understood *dog*. If necessary, point to the picture of the dog on the page.

4 Repeat the action rhyme 'Stand up and turn around' from Page 4.

Page 6 part 1

Active vocabulary
walk jump

1 Begin with a revision of the vocabulary from the previous lessons. Ask questions using colour and object cards. Ask questions about possessions with *my*, *your*, *his*, *her*.

2 Get the pupils to draw a picture of their own families in the blank frame. When they have finished ask them *Who is this?* eliciting answers like *(This is) my father*.

3 When you feel that pupils are answering effectively get one or two of them to ask the questions. If possible continue the action in groups.

4   Play the game 'Simon says' (see page 8), using actions learned up till now and *Bring me ...* or *Hold up ...* with colour and number cards and objects.

5   Repeat the action rhyme 'Stand up, turn around, sit down' from page 4.

6   Get the pupils to colour the new action rhyme.

7   Cut out and make the finger puppets from page C2. These will be worn on the finger for the action rhyme which follows. The puppets should be kept for later activities.

8   Act out the complete action rhyme in one single sequence. The pupils can do the actions (themselves or with puppets) and chant.

One, stand up. Two, turn around. Three, sit down. Four, walk. Five, jump. Six, sit down.

Stand up. Turn around. Sit down. Walk. Jump. Sit down.

Page 6   part 2

Active vocabulary
six   seven   eight   nine   ten   grey

1   Play the cassette for numbers six to ten. The pupils should join in.

> Six, seven, eight, nine, ten.
> Six, seven, eight, nine, ten.
> Six, seven, eight, nine, ten.
> Six, seven, eight, nine, ten.
>
> Ten, nine, eight, seven, six.
> Ten, nine, eight, seven, six.
> Ten, nine, eight, seven, six.
> Ten, nine, eight, seven, six.

2   Using fingers, number cards, and the blackboard, practise the numbers from one to ten.

3   The pupils complete the numbers by joining up the dotted lines, and colour them according to the instructions on the cassette. Teach *grey* before doing this.

> Number eight. It's black. [P]
> Number six. It's brown. [P]
> Number seven. It's grey. [P]
> Number ten. It's pink. [P]
> Number nine. It's purple. [P]

4   The pupils should cut out the numbers six to ten from page C6. These should be stuck on cards of the same size and the backs should be coloured black, white, pink, purple and grey.

5   Play the game 'Guessing' (see page 7) using the numbers one to ten. If time permits, pupils can continue playing in groups using their own cards.

6   The class could now (if time is available) be taught the game 'One potato, two potatoes' (see page 8). If there is too much disruption caused by playing with hand-slapping, pupils can hold up the correct number of fingers.

Page 7   part 1

Active vocabulary
parrot

1   Colour dictation. The pupils listen and colour the frame - at first only the frame - of the picture of the parrot. When they have coloured the frame they then use it as a key to colour the rest of the picture - i.e. all the number 3s on the picture should be coloured green.

> Number one. It's brown. [P]
> Number two. It's grey. [P]
> Number three. It's green. [P]
> Number four. It's orange. [P]
> Number five. It's pink. [P]
> Number six. It's purple. [P]
> Number seven. It's black. [P]
> Number eight. It's yellow. [P]
> Number nine. It's blue. [P]
> Number ten. It's red. [P]

2   Ask questions about the colours in the picture, for example *Number three. What colour is it?* Ask questions about all the numbers in this way.

3   The pupils now colour in the rest of the picture using the frame as a key.

4   Play the game 'Guessing', with colour and/or number cards. (See page 7 for instructions.)

Page 7 part 2

Active vocabulary

bird lamb cat Is there a … ? Yes there is
No there isn't

1   Teach or revise the animals using the cassette.

> ▱ Number one. It's a bird. (*bird noises*)[P]
> Number two. It's a lamb. (*bleating noises*)[P]
> Number three. It's a dog. (*barking noises*)[P]
> Number four. It's a cat. (*miaowing noises*)[P]

Practise the new vocabulary, asking questions like
What's number two?

2   Colour dictation. Play the cassette and colour the
animals.

> ▱ The bird is blue. [P]
> The lamb is white. [P]
> The dog is brown. [P]
> The cat is yellow and brown. [P]

3   Play the song 'Listen to the bird'. The pupils
should insert the noise appropriate to each
animal. Teach the first verse before going on to
the second.

> ▱ Listen to the bird go tweet, tweet, tweet.
> Listen to the lamb go bleat, bleat, bleat.
> Tweet, tweet, tweet. Bleat, bleat, bleat.
> Tweet, tweet. Bleat, bleat, bleat.
>
> Listen to the dog go bow, wow, wow.
> Listen to the cat go miaow, miaow, miaow.
> Bow, wow, wow. Miaow, miaow, miaow.
> Bow, wow. Miaow, miaow, miaow.
>
> Listen to the bird go (pupils insert the correct noise)
> Listen to the lamb go
>
> Listen to the dog go
> Listen to the cat go

4   Play the game 'What's in the bag?' using object
cards (see page 8). Choose six objects from the
following list; *pen, pencil, book, desk, paint, house,
balloon, car, bird, lamb, dog,* cat, any colour, and
the numbers from one to ten. Play together as a
class at the beginning, introducing the expressions *Yes, there is*, and *No, there isn't*. After
playing together as a class, this could be played in
groups, each group with a bag and objects.

5   If you are using the picture dictionary, pupils
should turn to page 39 and write in the vocabulary
(*dog* and *cat*).

Page 8 part 1

Active vocabulary

cakes biscuits sweets ice-cream chocolate
strawberries coffee tea I like Do you like?

1   Play the cassette to introduce the food
vocabulary. Encourage the pupils to repeat new
items by pausing after each.

> ▱ Look at number one! [P]They're sweets. [P]
> Look at number two! [P]They're strawberries. [P]
> Look at number three! [P]They're cakes. [P]
> Look at number four! [P]It's chocolate. [P]
> Look at number five! [P]It's ice-cream. [P]
> Look at number six! [P]They're biscuits. [P]

Consolidate the vocabulary by asking questions
using pictures or blackboard drawings.

2   Listen to the recording of Coco and Candy talking
about the food they like.

> ▱ Hello! I'm Coco.
> I like cakes.
> I like sweets.
> I like strawberries.
>
> Hello! I'm Candy.
> I like chocolate.
> I like ice-cream.
> I like biscuits.

Encourage pupils to repeat the phrases beginning
I like …

3   Ask the pupils questions about the food they have
learnt. Ask *Do you like …?* The pupils should
answer simply *Yes* or *No.*

4   If the pupils are managing well, move on to pair
work, with pupils asking and answering the
questions.

5   If the pupils are managing well, move on to the
use of the tag *Yes, I do.* Play the cassette
dialogue between Coco and Candy.

> ▱ Coco   Candy, do you like chocolate?
> Candy   Yes, I do.
> Coco   Do you like ice-cream?
> Candy   Yes, I do.

6   Ask these three questions *Do you like ice-cream?
Do you like strawberries? Do you like biscuits?*
giving the pupils time to reply *Yes, I do* or *No.*

7   Listen to and teach the rhyme 'I like coffee'.
Coffee and *tea* may need explaining.

📼 I like coffee,
You like tea.
Tea for you,
And coffee for me.

8   If you are using the picture dictionary, pupils should turn to pages 37 and 38 and write in the vocabulary (*cake, biscuits, sweets, strawberry, ice-cream, chocolate*).

Ten - stretch.
Eleven - stretch.
Twelve - stretch.
Thirteen - stretch.
Fourteen - stretch.
Fifteen - stretch.

Aim to get the pupils doing the rhyme and actions without the cassette.

Page 8   part 2

Active vocabulary
eleven twelve thirteen fourteen fifteen stretch

1   Listen to the numbers and teach them as previously.

📼 Eleven[P], twelve[P], thirteen[P], fourteen[P], fifteen[P]

2   Colour dictation.

📼 Look at number fourteen! Colour it blue. [P]
Look at number eleven! Colour it green. [P]
Look at number thirteen! Colour it orange. [P]
Look at number fifteen! Colour it purple. [P]
Look at number twelve! Colour it grey. [P]

3   The pupils cut out the numbers from page C4 and use them to make number cards. These should be used to play the game 'Guessing', (see page 7) using numbers one to fifteen. Particular attention should be paid to the pronunciation of *thirteen* and *fourteen*.

4   The pupils colour the small picture of Coco stretching. They choose their own colours.

5   Play the rhyme 'Stretching'. The pupils should stand up and stretch in time to the cassette and try and join in the rhyme. If standing and stretching is too disruptive this can be done sitting down, stretching the arms above the head.

📼 One - stretch.
Two - stretch.
Three - stretch.
Four - stretch.
Five - stretch.
Six - stretch.
Seven - stretch.
Eight - stretch.
Nine - stretch.

Page 9   part 1

Active vocabulary
hat candle trumpet birthday cake Yes, it is No, it isn't banana pear apple

1   Begin by revising the numbers one to fifteen, in sequence, in reverse order and out of sequence.

2   Play the cassette and teach the vocabulary.

📼 Look at number three! It's a trumpet. [P]
Look at number one! It's a hat. [P]
Look at number four! It's a birthday cake. [P]
Look at number two! It's a candle. [P]

Practise the new vocabulary, asking questions like this to the class and individual pupils. *Look at number two! What is it? Look at number four! What is it?*

3   As a class and then in pairs ask questions like *Is number three a cake?* The pupils should answer *Yes, it is* or *No, it isn't.*

4   Pupils colour the large picture according to the instructions. Teach *apple, pear* and *banana* before listening.

📼 One balloon is red. [P]
One balloon is blue.[P]
The bananas are yellow.[P]
Three pears are green.[P]
Four pears are yellow.[P]
The strawberries are red.[P]
One apple is green.[P]
Three apples are red.[P]
The cakes are pink and white.[P]

4   If you are using the picture dictionary, pupils should turn to page 38 and write in the vocabulary (*hat, candle, trumpet, banana, pear, apple*).

Page 9 part 2

Active vocabulary

How old are you? birthday he's she's

1 Ask one or two pupils *How old are you?* and get them to give their age. Set up a chain. The dialogue should go like this:

Pupil one *How old are you?*
Pupil two *I'm seven. How old are you?*
Pupil three *I'm eight. How old are you?*
Pupil four *I'm six. How old are you?* etc.

2 Ask questions about third persons using *How old is (name)?* Practise this in a chain as before.

Pupil one *How old is Tom?*
Pupil two *He's seven. How old is Katy?*
Pupil three *She's eight.* etc.

3 Song 'It's your birthday'. Let the pupils listen and then sing along with the cassette.

[cassette] It's your birthday here today
And we all want to say
Happy, happy, happy, happy day
It's your birthday here today.

Page 9 part 3

Active vocabulary

How many ... are there? There are ... touch nose toes

1 Listen to the cassette

[cassette] Candy Coco, how many pears are there?
Coco There are seven.
Candy How many balloons are there?
Coco There are two.

2 Ask pupils questions like *How many candles are there?* They should answer *There are ...*

3 Practise asking and answering *How many ...?* questions as a class and then in groups or pairs. Possible additional questions are *How many biscuits/cakes/balloons are there?*

4 Play the action rhyme 'Stand up and turn around'. The pupils join in and do the actions. Check that they understand the new vocabulary.

[cassette] Stand up, turn around
Touch your nose
And touch your toes.

Stand up, turn around
Touch your nose
And touch your toes.

Touch your nose, touch your toes.
Touch your nose, touch your toes.

Stand up, turn around
Touch your nose
And touch your toes.

5 Repeat the song 'Listen to the bird' (page 17).

6 If you are using the picture dictionary, pupils should turn to page 40 and write in the vocabulary (*nose* and *toes*)

Page 10

Active vocabulary

lemon orange milk orangeade No, I don't We like What do you like?

1 Play the cassette and teach or revise the vocabulary.

[cassette] Look at number five! What is it?
It's a lemon. [P]
Look at number one! What is it?
It's an orange. [P]
Look at number seven! What is it?
It's orangeade. [P]
Look at number eight! What is it?
It's a banana. [P]
Look at number two! What is it?
It's a strawberry. [P]
Look at number three! What is it?
It's an apple. [P]
Look at number four! What is it?
It's milk. [P]
Look at number six! What is it?
It's a pear. [P]

Try to get the pupils to repeat the *an* before vowels correctly, but don't worry about explanation.

2 Ask questions like these for the pupils to ask as a class or individually *Look at number five. What is it? Look at number one. What is it?*

3 Colour dictation.

> 🔲 Look at the lemon! Colour it yellow. [P]
> Look at the apple! Colour it red. [P]
> Look at the banana! Colour it yellow and brown. [P]
> Look at the strawberry! Colour it red. [P]
> Look at the orange! Colour it orange. [P]
> Look at the pear! Colour it green and yellow. [P]
> Look at the milk! Colour it white. [P]

4 Now ask the pupils questions, building up to the following type of dialogue, using the food on page 10. Try and get the pupils to use *Yes, I do*, and *No, I don't*, where appropriate.

Teacher	*Number three. What is it?*
Pupil	*It's an apple.*
Teacher	*What colour is it?*
Pupil	*It's red.*
Teacher	*Do you like apples?*
Pupil	*Yes, I do* or *No, I don't.*

With a very confident and able class this dialogue could be practised in pairs.

5 Song 'I like apples'. Let the pupils listen and then sing along with the cassette.

> 🔲 A   I like apples, I like apples.
> B   I like pears, I like pears.
> A&B   We like apples and pears.
>
> A   I like oranges, I like oranges.
> B   I like lemons, I like lemons.
> A&B   We like oranges and lemons.

6 The pupils turn to page C4 and cut out six illustrations of things which they like. They stick these in the spaces at the bottom of page 10. Then ask the pupils individually, for example *Mary, what do you like?* Pupils will answer *I like ...* according to what they have stuck in their books. Keep the unused illustrations for flashcards.

7 If you are using the picture dictionary, pupils should turn to page 38 and write in the vocabulary (*lemon*, *orange*, *milk*, *orangeade*).

Page 11   part 1

1 Pupils complete the drawings of the apples, bananas, pencils, cakes, strawberries and books and write the number of objects in the space to the right.

2 Revise *there are* and numbers by asking questions like *How many apples are there? How many bananas are there?* The pupils should answer *There are ...* and give the number. Then play the colour dictation.

> 🔲 There are three green apples and three red apples. [P]
> There are six yellow bananas and four green bananas. [P]
> There are two blue pencils. [P]
> There is one pink pencil. [P]
> There are three black pencils. [P]
> There is one brown pencil. [P]
> There are two orange pencils. [P]
> There are three pink cakes and one white cake. [P]
> There is one green strawberry and there are two red strawberries. [P]
> There is one red book and there is one orange book. [P]

3 Ask questions like these, either to the class as a whole or to individuals *How many pink cakes are there? How many red strawberries are there?* Continue, if possible, in groups or pairs.

Page 11   part 2

Active vocabulary
    ball   Coco's

1 Pupils should listen to the cassette, look at the numbers and draw the additional items necessary. For example, there should be seven pears, so pupils should draw three extra ones. Check that the pupils understand *ball*.

> 🔲 There are seven pears. Draw the pears. [P]
> There are ten balloons. Draw the balloons. [P]
> There are nine balls. Draw the balls. [P]
> There are six sweets. Draw the sweets. [P]
> There are eight ice-creams. Draw the ice-creams. [P]
> There are three houses. Draw the houses. [P]
> There are five candles. Draw the candles. [P]
> There are two cars. Draw the car. [P]
> There are four hats. Draw the hat. [P]
> There is one trumpet. Draw the trumpet. [P]

2 Pupils colour the pictures, choosing their own colours. Then play the dialogue between Coco and Candy.

> 🔲 Candy   Coco, what colour are your ice-creams?
> Coco   They're pink and white.

Then ask questions like *What colour are your hats? What colour are your candles?* for the pupils to answer according to what colours they have used. As a class, and then in pairs, pupils should ask and answer more questions of this type.

3   Using the picture at the bottom of the page revise by asking questions like *Who's this?* and eliciting the answer *It's Coco.* Then introduce the use of the possessive *'s*, with exchanges like *Who's this? It's Coco's father.* Revise *How old are you?*

4   Repeat the rhyme 'My family' from page 5.

5   If you are using the picture dictionary, pupils should turn to page 38 and write in the vocabulary (*ball*).

5   If you are using the picture dictionary, pupils should turn to pages 38 and 39 and write in the vocabulary (*window, blackboard, chair, door, table*)

Page 12   part 1

Active vocabulary
window   blackboard   chair   door   table

1   Listen to the cassette to present the new vocabulary.

   Look at number eleven! It's a window. [P]
Look at number fourteen! It's a door. [P]
Look at number fifteen! It's a table. [P]
Look at number thirteen! It's a chair. [P]
Look at number twelve! It's a blackboard. [P]

Check that the new vocabulary has been understood by asking questions (*What is it?*)and pointing to objects in the classroom.

2   Get the pupils to ask and answer questions themselves, creating exchanges like *What is it? It's a chair.* etc.

3   Colour dictation.

The door is red. [P]
The table is blue. [P]
The window is green. [P]
The chair is yellow. [P]
The blackboard is grey. [P]

4   Listen to the following dialogue. Pupils can then invent and practise variations in pairs.

Coco   Look at number fourteen! What is it?
Candy   It's a door.
Coco   Is it blue?
Candy   Yes, it's blue. It's a blue door.

Page 12   part 2

Active vocabulary
sixteen   seventeen   eighteen   nineteen   twenty

1   Teach the numbers as in the preceding lessons.

Sixteen,[P] seventeen,[P] eighteen,[P] nineteen, [P]twenty.[P]

2   Pupils colour the numbers with the colours of their choice. Alternatively, the colours can be dictated to them as follows *Look at number eighteen! Colour it pink. Look at number twenty! Colour it purple. Look at number nineteen! Colour it yellow. Look at number sixteen! Colour it orange. Look at number seventeen! Colour it brown.*

3   Practise counting from one to twenty and from twenty back to one. This should be done around the class.

4   Play the cassette for the stretching rhyme (see page 18) including the new numbers.

Sixteen - stretch.
Seventeen - stretch.
Eighteen - stretch.
Nineteen - stretch.
Twenty - stretch.

5   Cut out and make cards of the numbers from page C7 and play the game 'Guessing' (see page 7) using numbers from one to twenty.

Page 13

Active Vocabulary
telephone

1   The pupils colour four of the empty squares at the top of the page with colours of their choice. In the other four squares they write any number they choose from one to twenty, There should be only one colour or number per square.

2 Play 'Bingo'. To do this the teacher should have all the possible colour cards and number cards in a bag (or face down on the desk) and pull them out one by one. The pupils cross out those on their own grids which are called. The winner is the first pupil who has crossed out all eight squares. One of the pupils can also take the role of caller.

3 The pupils colour the ten objects in the central grid with their own colours. It is possible to play Bingo again using these, calling combinations of object and colour like *a red pencil*, *a blue telephone*. This will take a long time, however. Check that *telephone* has been understood.

4 Play the dialogue.

[cassette]	Coco	What colour's your trumpet, Candy?
	Candy	It's yellow. [P]
	Coco	What colour's your telephone?
	Candy	It's pink. [P]
	Coco	What colour's your chair?
	Candy	It's red. [P]
	Coco	What colour's your pencil?
	Candy	It's purple. [P]
	Coco	What colour's your cake?
	Candy	It's white. [P]
	Coco	What colour's your apple?
	Candy	It's red and green. [P]
	Coco	What colour's your balloon?
	Candy	It's blue. [P]
	Coco	What colour's your book?
	Candy	It's black. [P]
	Coco	What colour's your strawberry?
	Candy	It's red. [P]
	Coco	What colour's your ice-cream?
	Candy	It's pink and yellow. [P]

5 Ask questions of the type *What colour's your balloon?* If possible let the pupils continue with pair or group practice.

6 The pupils cut out the picture from the bottom of page C7 and stick it at the bottom of page 13. They then listen to and join in on the action rhyme 'This is an apple' , pointing to the objects.

> [cassette] This is an apple
> This is a ball
> This is the cat that sits on the wall.

7 If you are using the picture dictionary, pupils should turn to page 39 and write in the vocabulary (*telephone*).

Page 14   part 1

Active vocabulary
What's your telephone number?

1 The pupils listen to the dialogues and follow the telephone wires joining the characters to their telephones.

[cassette]	Candy	What's your telephone number, Coco?
	Coco	It's 9 8 1 0 7.
	Coco	What's your telephone number, Candy?
	Candy	It's 4 3 2 0 6 1.

2 When the pupils have listened two or three times, begin asking them questions of the type *What's your telephone number, dog?*

3 Get the pupils to repeat the question *What's your telephone number?* and to answer it. Tell them to invent a telephone number if they don't have one or if they don't know it.

4 Get some pupils to act out a dialogue using these questions in front of the class. Then, if possible, move on to pair or group work.

5 Pupils write the correct telephone numbers under the telephones. Ask them questions of the type *Look at the dog! What's his telephone number?* Pupils then ask and answer similar questions working in groups or pairs.

6 Listen to and sing the song 'What's your telephone number?'

> [cassette] What's your telephone number?
> What's your telephone number?
> It's 54321.
>
> What's your telephone number?
> What's your telephone number?
> It's 92031.
>
> What's your telephone number?
> What's your telephone number?
> It's 38962.

Page 14   part 2

Active Vocabulary
It's me   How are you?   I'm fine thanks

1 The pupils listen to the telephone call.

(Ring ring)

Candy	Hello.
Mary	Hello Candy. It's me, Mary.
Candy	Hello Mary. How are you?
Mary	I'm fine thanks, and you.
Candy	I'm fine thanks.
Mary	Goodbye.
Candy	Goodbye.

2 After listening, play the dialogue phrase by phrase and get the pupils to repeat. Then, build up sections of dialogue using the pupils 's own names. For example:

> *Hello.*
> *Hello, Susan. It's me, Kim.*
> *Hello Kim. How are you?*

then:

> *Hello Kim, How are you?*
> *I'm fine thanks. And you?*
> *I'm fine, thanks.*
> *Goodbye.*
> *Goodbye.*

If possible, pupils should move on to acting out the dialogues in pairs, using their own names.

3 At the bottom of the page the pupils draw a picture of themselves and write their telephone number. If time permits 'chain' questions and answers around the class.

Pupil 1	*What's your telephone number?*
Pupil 2	*It's … … … … … What's your telephone number?*
Pupil 3	*It's … … … … … What's your telephone number?*
Pupil 4	*Its … (etc)*

Page 15 part 1

Active vocabulary
bicycle   kite   whistle   teddy bear   box

1 Using the cassette and, if necessary, flash cards and blackboard drawings, teach the new vocabulary at the top of the page.

Number four. What is it? It's a whistle. [P]
Number six. What is it? It's a banana. [P]

Number three. What is it? It's a ball. [P]
Number eight. What is it? It's a cake. [P]
Number seven. What is it? It's a pencil. [P]
Number two. What is it? It's an ice-cream. [P]
Number five. What is it? It's a bicycle. [P]
Number one. What is it? It's a pear. [P]

2 Practise the vocabulary by asking questions around the class of the type *Number four. What is it?* Continue practising with pair or group work.

3 Teach the new vocabulary in the second part of the page and practise it as before.

Number sixteen. What is it? It's a box. [P]
Number eleven. What is it? It's a lemon. [P]
Number fourteen. What is it? It's a chair. [P]
Number ten. What is it? It's a balloon. [P]
Number fifteen. What is it? It's an apple. [P]
Number twelve. What is it? It's a teddy bear. [P]
Number nine. What is it? It's a kite. [P]
Number thirteen. What is it? It's a book. [P]

Practise the vocabulary by asking questions of the type *Number sixteen. What is it?*

4 If you are using the picture dictionary, pupils should turn to page 39 and write in the vocabulary (*whistle, bicycle, box, kite, teddy bear*).

Page 15 part 2

Active vocabulary
He's got   She's got   Has he/she got …?

1 Play the cassette.

Look at Coco!
He's got a ball. [P]
He's got a pear. [P]
He's got a whistle. [P]
He's got a pencil. [P]
He's got a cake. [P]
He's got a banana. [P]

Look at Candy!
She's got a book. [P]
She's got a lemon. [P]
She's got a kite. [P]
She's got a box. [P]
She's got a balloon. [P]
She's got a teddy bear. [P]

Ensure that pupils have understood and explain where necessary.

2   Listen to the questions and answers.

> Has Coco got a bicycle? [P] Yes, he has. [P]
> Has Coco got a teddy bear? [P] No, he hasn't. [P]
>
> Has Candy got a teddy bear? [P] Yes, she has. [P]
> Has Candy got a pencil? [P] No, she hasn't. [P]

Continue asking questions of the same type. Then get the pupils to repeat both the question forms and the answers. Don't worry too much about the tags (*he has, he hasn't*).

3   Ask questions of the type *Has Candy got an ice-cream?* The pupils should answer *Yes* or *No*.

4   Working first as a class, then, if possible, in pairs or groups, ask and answer questions about Coco's and Candy's possessions.

5   Teach the vocabulary *eyes* and *fat*, and listen to and repeat the rhyme 'My cat'. The pupils should cut out the picture of the cat from page C7 and stick it on page 15.

> I've got a big white cat.
> His eyes are blue
> And he's very fat.

6   If time permits, the pupils colour the objects the colours of their choice.

Page 16   part 1

Active vocabulary
drum puppet doll boat train Have you got ...? Yes, I have   No, I haven't

1   Teach the vocabulary at the top of the page in the usual way.

> Number sixteen. What is it?[P] It's a boat. [P]
> Number fourteen. What is it? [P] It's a puppet. [P]
> Number twenty. What is it? [P] It's a teddy bear. [P]
> Number seventeen. What is it? [P] It's a trumpet. [P]
> Number fifteen. What is it? [P] It's a ball. [P]
> Number nineteen. What is it? [P] It's a train. [P]
> Number eighteen. What is it? [P] It's a whistle. [P]
> Number thirteen. What is it? [P] It's a drum. [P]

Ask questions of the type *Number sixteen. What is it?* to consolidate the new vocabulary.

2   Colour dictation.

> Look at the drum! [P] Colour it red and blue. [P]
> Look at the teddy bear! [P] Colour it yellow and brown. [P]
> Look at the whistle! [P] Colour it grey. [P]
> Look at the trumpet! [P] Colour it yellow. [P]
> Look at the ball! [P] Colour it green and orange. [P]
> Look at the train! [P] Colour it green and black. [P]
> Look at the puppet! [P] Colour it red and white. [P]
> Look at the boat! [P] Colour it blue and white. [P]

3   When the pupils have finished colouring, continue asking questions of the type *What colour's the boat? What number is it?* If possible, move on to group work with the pupils asking the questions.

4   Play the cassette. The pupils should listen and repeat the phrases. Ensure that they have understood.

> Have you got a boat? Yes, I have. [P]
> Have you got a teddy bear? No, I haven't. [P]

5   Then continue with the pupils answering for themselves. Ensure that they understand that their answers should be their own. Ask questions like *Have you got a boat? Have you got a teddy bear?*

6   Once the pupils can manage both questions and answers, move on from class to group or pair work.

7   Song 'I've got a drum'. Let the pupils listen and then sing along with the cassette. They should pretend to play the instruments.

> I've got a drum.
> I've got a drum.
>
> I've got a trumpet.
> I've got a trumpet.
>
> I've got a whistle.
> I've got a whistle.
>
> I've got a drum.
> I've got a drum.
>
> I've got a trumpet.
> I've got a trumpet.
>
> I've got a whistle.
> I've got a whistle.

8   If you are using the picture dictionary, pupils should turn to page 39 and write in the vocabulary (*drum, puppet, doll, boat, train*).

Page 16   part 2

Active vocabulary
big small short tall or

1 Teach the four adjectives *big, small, short, tall,* using the illustration at the bottom of the page and the cassette. Use gestures to indicate the meaning of the adjectives. Pupils should repeat each phrase.

> ▱ Look at the boat! [P] It's big! [P]
> Look at the whistle! [P] It's small! [P]
> Look at the doll! [P] It's short! [P]
> Look at the puppet! [P] It's tall! [P]

2 Pupils listen to and answer the questions.

> ▱ Is the boat big or small? [P]
> Is the whistle big or small? [P]
> Is the doll short or tall? [P]
> Is the puppet short or tall? [P]

Continue asking questions of this type using objects in the classroom and teach the pupils to ask them. If possible move on to group or pair work.

3 Song 'My toys'.

> ▱ My boat's big,
> My whistle's small,
> My doll's short,
> And my puppet's tall.
>
> My boat's big,
> My whistle's small,
> My doll's short,
> And my puppet is tall.

Page 17 part 1

1 Colour dictation.

> ▱ Look at the ball! [P] Colour it red. [P]
> Look at the trumpet! [P] Colour it blue. [P]
> Look at the train! [P] Colour it yellow. [P]
> Look at the teddy bear! [P] Colour it yellow. [P]

The pupils then colour the other objects at the top of the page with colours of their choice.

2 The pupils listen and answer the questions.

> ▱ What colour's your train? [P] It's yellow.
> What colour's your ball? [P] It's red.
> What colour's your trumpet? [P] It's blue.

Continue asking questions of the same type

3 Ensure that the pupils can ask as well as answer

the questions and move on from class to pair or group work.

Page 17 part 2

Active vocabulary
run   close

1 The pupils cut out the pictures of Coco and Candy from page C3 and stick them over the pictures on page 17.

2 The pupils listen to the cassette and do the actions in the action rhymes 'Walk, run, jump' and 'Turn around, sit down'. If necessary this can be done with finger puppets.

> ▱ One, turn around. Two, sit down. Three, open your book.
> Four, close your book.
> One, turn around. Two, sit down. Three, open your book.
> Four, close your book.

3 Teach the numbers twenty-one to twenty-five, as before.

> ▱ Twenty-one, [P] twenty-two, [P] twenty-three, [P] twenty-four, [P] twenty-five. [P]

4 Colour dictation.

> ▱ Number twenty-three. [P] It's grey. [P]
> Number twenty-five. [P] It's green. [P]
> Number twenty-one. [P] It's orange. [P]
> Number twenty-four. [P] It's blue. [P]
> Number twenty-two. [P] It's purple. [P]

5 Write numbers 1 - 25 on the blackboard out of sequence. Point to any number and call out the name of a pupil. The pupil has to say the number as quickly as possible.

6 Play the game 'Guessing' (see page 7) using numbers one to twenty-five.

Page 18 part 1

1 The pupils cut out from page C3 eight articles which they possess or which they would like to possess. They stick these on the squares in the grid at the top of the page. They draw a picture of themselves in the frame.

2 Ask the pupils questions like *Jane, have you got a book?* If Jane has a picture of a book stuck on her grid she answers *Yes, I have.* If not, she says *No, I haven't.* Once the pupils have understood the procedure they can play this in groups or in pairs.

3 Play 'Bingo' using all the vocabulary in the cut-out section, the pupils using their grids as cards.

Page 18 part 2

1 The pupils cut out and stick in six items which they think Coco might possess. This time the questions will be *Has he got ...? Yes, he has/No, he hasn't.* Once again 'Bingo' could be played.

2 The pupils cut out and stick in six items which they think Candy might possess. This time the questions will be *Has she got ...? Yes, she has/No, she hasn't.* Once again 'Bingo' could be played.

3 Let the pupils choose a song to sing, or do the rhyme 'Stretching' from numbers one to twenty-five.

Page 19 part 1

1 The pupils listen to the cassette and follow the lines to see who has what.

> Number one.[P] What's he got? He's got a ball.[P]
> Number two.[P] What's she got? She's got a trumpet.[P]
> *Now you answer.*
> Number one.[P] What's he got?[P]
> Number two.[P] What's she got?[P]
> Number three.[P] What's he got?[P]
> Number four.[P] What's he got?[P]
> Number five.[P] What's she got?[P]
> Number six.[P] What's she got?[P]

2 Ask the pupils questions of the type *Has number one got a drum?* The pupils answer *Yes, he has* or *No he hasn't.* If possible continue with these questions and answers in groups or pairs.

3 If time is available, pupils can colour the illustration.

4 Play the game 'Simon says' (see page 8) using all the actions learnt up till now.

Page 19 part 2

Active vocabulary
> on near in floor corner where

1 Teach the word floor. Teach the prepositions on, in, and near. Use classroom objects to do this. For example, hold up a book, for the pupils to see, then place it on a desk and say *The book is on the desk*. Then the pupils listen to the cassette and repeat.

> The boat is on the table. [P]
> The car is on the floor. [P]
> The dog is near the door. [P]
> The chair is in the corner. [P]

The pupils now listen to and repeat the questions and answers and then answer the questions themselves.

> Is the boat on the table? [P] Yes it is. [P]
> Is the car on the floor? [P] Yes it is. [P]

2 Continue asking questions of the same type. Introduce negatives as well like *Is the car on the table? No it isn't.*

3 The pupils continue in groups, asking and answering questions of the same type.

4 Continue with the illustration on the right.

> Two boats are on the table. [P]
> Two chairs are in the corner. [P]
> Two dogs are near the door. [P]
> Two cars are on the floor. [P]

The pupils should listen to and repeat the question and answer. Then ask them more questions of the same type, including negatives *Are the boats on the table? Yes, they are. Are the cars on the table? No, they aren't.*

5 The pupils can continue in groups, asking and answering questions of the same type.

6 Song 'The boat is on the table'. The pupils point to the appropriate object as they sing.

> The boat is on the table.
> The car is on the floor.
> The chair is in the corner.
> And the dog is near the door.
> Two boats are on the table.
> Two cars are on the floor.
> Two chairs are in the corner.
> And two dogs are near the door.

Page 20 part 1

Active vocabulary
under

1 Teach *under* in the same way as the prepositions were taught in the previous lesson.

2 The pupils listen to the cassette. Explain to them that they must write the correct number in the picture to which it refers. For example, they should write 1 in the middle picture (they will also have to write 5 in this picture).

> [cassette] Number one. [P] The cake is on the table. [P]
> Number two. [P] The book is under the table. [P]
> Number three. [P] The ball is on the desk. [P]
> Number four. [P] The car is under the table. [P]
> Number five. [P] The candle is on the cake. [P]
> Number six. [P] The boat is in the box. [P]

3 The pupils now listen to and repeat the questions and answers. Then ask them more questions of the same type.

> [cassette] Where's the boat? [P] It's in the box. [P]
> Where's the ball? [P] It's on the table. [P]
> Where's the candle? [P] It's on the cake. [P]
> Now you answer.
> Where's the boat? [P]
> Where's the ball? [P]

4 The pupils listen and repeat the dialogue. If they are managing well, they could continue inventing dialogues of this type in pairs.

> *Is the ball on the box?*
> *No, it isn't.*
> *Where is it?*
> *It's on the desk.*

Page 20 part 2

Active vocabulary
Have they got ...? Yes, they have No, they haven't twenty-six twenty-seven twenty-eight twenty-nine thirty

1 Colour dictation.

> [cassette] There are four purple pencils. [P]
> There are four grey pencils. [P]
> There are two red pencils and two pink pencils. [P]
> There are three blue and white balls. [P]
> There are three orange and yellow balls. [P]
> There are two purple and pink balls. [P]
> There are three brown teddy bears and two yellow teddy bears. [P]
> There is one blue book and one orange book. [P]
> There is one pink and white cake. [P]
> There are two yellow cakes. [P]

Remember to pause the cassette to give the pupils time to colour.

2 Pupils listen to and repeat the questions and answers, then answer the questions for themselves.

> [cassette] Look at Coco and Candy!
> Have they got fourteen pencils? [P]
> No, they haven't. [P]
> How many pencils have they got? [P]
> They've got twelve. [P]
>
> Have they got three cakes? [P]
> Yes, they have. [P]

Ask more questions of the same type. Then play the following questions.

> [cassette] How many balls have they got? [P]
> How many pencils have they got? [P]
>
> How many blue and white balls have they got? [P]
> How many brown teddy bears have they got? [P]

Ask more questions of the same type.

3 Continue asking questions of this type. Then practise asking and answering questions first with the whole class, then, if possible, in groups or pairs.

4 Teach and practise the numbers twenty-six to thirty.

> [cassette] Twenty-six, [P] twenty-seven, [P] twenty-eight, [P] twenty-nine, [P] thirty. [P]

5 Pupils colour the numbers freely. They should then ask one another about the colours they have used, asking questions like *What colour's twenty-eight?*

6 Then practise asking and answering questions of the same type, first with the whole class, then, if possible, in groups or pairs.

Page C1

This page is intended for use at Christmas, and may therefore be used at the point during the course when Christmas is at hand. The pupils can cut out the Christmas tree and can then stick the decorations on. The base of the Christmas tree can be rolled round to make a trunk so that the tree stands up.

Page C10

This page should be used near Easter. The basket should be cut up and folded. The various decorations can be stuck inside or outside.

Page 21 part 1

Active vocabulary
rectangle circle triangle heart star square shape

1   Using the cassette, teach and practise the new vocabulary.

> Look at number one! [P] It's a rectangle. [P]
> Look at number two! [P] It's a circle. [P]
> Look at number three! [P] It's a triangle. [P]
> Look at number four! [P] It's a heart. [P]
> Look at number five! [P] It's a star. [P]
> Look at number six! [P] It's a square. [P]

Ask questions of the type *Number four. What is it?*

2   Play the cassette and listen to the example. The pupils should then answer more questions of the same type.

> Is number three a square? [P]
> No, it isn't. It's a triangle. [P]

Continue asking and answering questions of this type, first with the whole class, then, if possible, in groups or pairs.

3   Colour dictation.

> Look at the circle! [P] It's blue. [P]
> Look at the square! [P] It's orange. [P]
> Look at the star! [P] It's yellow. [P]
> Look at the heart! [P] It's red. [P]
> Look at the rectangle! [P] It's green. [P]
> Look at the triangle! [P] It's purple. [P]

4   Get the pupils to colour the drawing of the car and bicycle and find the hidden shapes. The shapes should be coloured the same colours as in the colour dictation.

Page 21 part 2

Active vocabulary
thirty-one thirty-two thirty-three thirty-four thirty-five

1   Teach the pupils this as an action rhyme. Teach the word *point*. The pupils join in and do the actions. They should also cut out and stick in the pictures from page C2.

> *Open your book and close your book.*
> *Touch your nose and touch your toes.*
> *Point to the window and point to the door.*
>
> *Open your book and close your book.*
> *Touch your nose and touch your toes.*
> *Point to the window and point to the door.*

2   Listen to and teach the numbers thirty-one to thirty-five.

> Thirty-one, [P] thirty-two, [P] thirty-three, [P] thirty-four, [P] thirty-five. [P]

3   The pupils colour the numbers with colours of their own choice. Ask questions like *What colour is number thirty-three?* Continue asking questions of this type. Then practise asking and answering, first with the whole class, then, if possible, in groups or pairs.

4   Play the game 'Guessing' (see page 7) using numbers up to thirty-five.

5   Play the game 'Simon says' (see page 8) using verbs from previous units and all those used on this page *close, open, point, touch, bring.*

Page 22

Active vocabulary
skirt T-shirt socks dress jeans shirt shoes thirty-six thirty-seven thirty-eight thirty-nine forty

1 Play the cassette to teach the vocabulary and then teach and practise using pictures and also the clothes which you and the pupils are wearing. You can walk around the classroom pointing to articles of clothing and asking *What's this? What are these?* and also *What colour is it/are they?*

> Look at number twenty-three! [P] It's a T-shirt. [P]
> Look at number twenty-five! [P] They're jeans. [P]
> Look at number twenty-one! [P] It's a shirt. [P]
> Look at number twenty-four! [P] It's a dress. [P]
> Look at number twenty-two! [P] It's a skirt. [P]
> Look at number twenty-seven! [P] They're socks. [P]
> Look at number twenty-six! [P] They're shoes. [P]

2 Colour dictation.

> What colour are her jeans? [P] They're blue. [P]
> What colour are her shoes? [P]They're blue and white. [P]
> What colour is her shirt? [P] It's yellow. [P]
> What colour is her T-shirt? [P] It's purple. [P]
> What colour are her socks? [P] They're red and green. [P]
> What colour is her skirt? [P] It's orange. [P]
> What colour is her dress? [P] It's pink and black. [P]

3 When the pupils have finished colouring, play the following questions, giving the pupils time to respond.

> Is her T-shirt green?[P] No, it isn't. It's purple. [P]
> Are her shoes blue and white? [P] Yes they are. [P]

Continue asking questions of this type. Then practise asking and answering questions of this type first with the whole class, then, if possible, in groups or pairs.

4 Ask questions of the type *Have you got a shirt?* depending on what the pupils are wearing. Continue asking questions of this type, first with the whole class, then, if possible, in groups or pairs. Move on to questions like *Is your T-shirt blue?* or *Have you got black shoes?*

5 Teach and practise the numbers. The pupils can colour the numbers and then ask and answer questions about their colours.

> Thirty-six, [P] thirty-seven, [P] thirty-eight, [P] thirty-nine, [P] forty. [P]

6 Song 'My clothes'. Let the pupils listen and then sing along with the cassette.

> My shirt is orange,
> My jeans are blue,
> My T-shirt's white
> And my shoes are, too.

7 If you are using the picture dictionary, pupils should turn to page 40 and write in the vocabulary (*dress*, *skirt*, *T-shirt*, *shirt*, *socks*, *shoes*, *jeans*).

Page 23

Active vocabulary
gloves sweater trousers scarf forty-one
forty-two forty-three forty-four forty-five

1 Play the cassette to teach the vocabulary and then teach and practise, using pictures and also the clothes which you and the pupils are wearing. You can walk around the classroom pointing to articles of clothing and asking *What's this? What are these?* and also *What colour is it/are they?*

> Look at number thirty-four! [P] It's a sweater. [P]
> Look at number thirty-one! [P] It's a shirt. [P]
> Look at number thirty-five! [P] They're trousers. [P]
> Look at number thirty-six! [P] It's a T-shirt. [P]
> Look at number thirty! [P] They're gloves. [P]
> Look at number twenty-eight! [P] It's a hat. [P]
> Look at number thirty-two! [P] It's a scarf.[P]
> Look at number thirty-three! [P] They're shoes. [P]
> Look at number twenty-nine! [P] They're socks. [P]

2 Colour dictation.

> Look at Coco!
> What colour is his shirt? [P] It's red. [P]
> What colour are his trousers? [P] They're green. [P]
> What colour is his sweater? [P] It's blue. [P]
> What colour are his shoes? [P]
>   They're orange and black. [P]
> What colour are his socks? [P]
>   They're green and purple. [P]
> What colour is his hat? [P] It's red and blue. [P]
> What colour are his gloves? [P] They're brown. [P]
> What colour is his scarf? [P] It's red and blue. [P]
> What colour is his T-shirt? [P] It's yellow. [P]

3 When the pupils have finished colouring, play the following questions, giving the pupils time to respond.

> Is his T-shirt green? [P] No, it isn't. It's yellow. [P]
> Are his shoes orange and black? [P] Yes they are. [P]

Continue asking questions of the same type.

4 Ask questions of the following type, depending on what the pupils are wearing *Have you got a shirt? Have you got sweater?* Continue asking questions of answering questions, first with the

whole class, then, if possible, in groups or pairs. Move on to questions such as *Is your T-shirt blue?* or *Have you got black shoes?*

5   The pupils cut out the dolls from page C8. These should be glued to cardboard to make them stiff enough to stand up. They can now cut out the clothes and dress the dolls. When this has been done, ask the pupils to describe what their dolls are wearing. They should say something like *Look at my doll. He's got a red shirt and blue jeans.*

Then practise asking and answering questions of this type first with the whole class, then, if possible, in groups or pairs.

6   Describe the clothes of one of the pupils in the class, without saying who it is. The other pupils have to guess who it is. If there is sufficient time, the pupils could also do this together in groups.

7   Teach and practise the numbers. The pupils can colour the numbers and then ask and answer questions about their colours?

    [cassette] Forty-one, [P] forty-two, [P] forty-three, [P] forty-four, [P] forty-five. [P]

8   Colour dictation.

    [cassette] Look at number forty-three. [P] It's purple. [P]
    Look at number forty-five. [P] It's yellow. [P]
    Look at number forty-one. [P] It's blue. [P]
    Look at number forty-four. [P] It's orange. [P]
    Look at number forty-two. [P] It's pink. [P]

9   Write numbers on the board, or use flashcards. Get the pupils to call out numbers as they appear.

10 If you are using the picture dictionary, pupils should turn to page 40 and write in the vocabulary (*gloves*, *sweater*, *trousers*, *scarf*).

Page 24   part 1

1   The pupils listen to the cassette and write the numbers next to the appropriate illustrations. It may be useful to revise some of the vocabulary before doing this.

    [cassette] Number one. [P] The chair is under the window. [P]
    Number two. [P] The dog is under the table. [P]
    Number eight. [P] The boat is on the table. [P]
    Number five. [P] The doll is on the chair. [P]
    Number four. [P] The pen is in the box. [P]

Number six. [P] The cat is under the table. [P]
Number seven. [P] The star is in the square. [P]
Number three. [P] The triangle is in the circle. [P]

2   Make statements of the type *The star is in the square*. The pupils should answer with the appropriate number.

3   With a more confident class, a chain could be set up, asking and answering questions on this pattern.

    | Pupil 1 | *Number two.* |
    | Pupil 2 | *The dog is under the table.* |
    | | *Number six.* |
    | Pupil 3 | *The cat is under the table.* |
    | | *Number five.* etc. |

This could be continued in pairs. Pupils could also colour the objects and questions about colour could be included.

4   Play the song 'Take your pen'. Let the pupils listen and then sing along with the cassette. They should do the actions as they sing.

    [cassette] Take your pen, take your pen!
    Put it in the box! Put it in the box!
    Put it in the box!

    Take your book, take your book!
    Put it on the desk! Put it on the desk!
    Put it on the desk!

    Take your pencil, take your pencil!
    Put it on the floor! Put it on the floor!
    Put it on the floor!

    My pen is in the box. My book is on the desk.
    My pencil's on the floor. My pencil's on the floor.
    My pencil's on the floor.

Page 24   part 2

Active vocabulary
kangaroo tiger seal penguin zoo

1   Teach the vocabulary using the cassette and the pictures in the book. Plastic animals or flashcards could also be used.

    [cassette] Look at number eleven! [P] What is it? It's a tiger. [P]
    Look at number ten! [P] What is it? It's a parrot. [P]
    Look at number three! [P] What is it? It's a kangaroo. [P]
    Look at number fourteen! [P] What is it? It's a penguin. [P]
    Look at number seven! [P] What is it? It's a seal. [P]

Ask questions of the type *Look at number eleven! What is it?*

2 Colour dictation.

> 🔊 Look at the kangaroo! [P] It's brown. [P]
> Look at the tiger! [P] It's black and yellow. [P]
> Look at the parrot! [P] It's red, green and yellow. [P]
> Look at the seal! [P] It's black. [P]
> Look at the penguin! [P] It's black and white. [P]
> Look at the sun! [P] It's orange. [P]

3 For this game you will need cards showing the following animals; dog, cat, lamb, bird, parrot, tiger, kangaroo, seal, penguin. These can be made from magazine pictures or from the pictures in *Toy Box*. Revise the vocabulary on the cards. One pupil then comes to the front of the class and, without the others seeing, chooses a card. The others then have to guess what animal the pupil is, asking questions like *Are you a penguin?* The pupil should answer *Yes, I am* or *No, I'm not*. When a pupil has correctly guessed the answer it becomes their turn to be an animal. This game can also be played in groups.

4 If you are using the picture dictionary, pupils should turn to pages 40 and 41 and write in the vocabulary (*tiger, seal, kangaroo, parrot, penguin*).

Page 25 part 1

Active vocabulary
tent flagpole giraffe elephant monkey snake crocodile lion

1 Teach *tent* and *flagpole*. Revise *flag* and the shapes used in the colour dictation.

2 Play the colour dictation. They colour the picture according to the symbols. For example, all the squares will be coloured orange. Pause after each sentence to give pupils time to start colouring, but once the basic pattern is understood the colouring can be finished later.

> 🔊 The squares are orange. [P]
> The circles are yellow. [P]
> The hearts are red. [P]
> The triangles are blue. [P]
> The rectangles are brown. [P]
> The stars are green. [P]

3 Ask questions of the type *What colour are the hearts?*

4 Teach the new animal vocabulary using the

cassette and the pictures in the book. Plastic animals or flashcards could also be used.

> 🔊 Look at number eight! [P] It's an elephant. [P]
> Look at number two! [P] It's a lion. [P]
> Look at number five! [P] It's a crocodile. [P]
> Look at number six! [P] It's a giraffe. [P]
> Look at number nine! [P] It's a monkey. [P]
> Look at number four! [P] It's a snake. [P]

Ask questions of the type *Number two. What is it?* Continue asking questions of this type. Then practise asking and answering questions first with the whole class, then, if possible, in groups or pairs.

5 Colour dictation.

> 🔊 The elephant is pink. [P] It's a pink elephant. [P]
> The snake is orange and blue. [P] It's an orange and blue snake. [P]
> The crocodile is green and yellow. [P] It's a green and yellow crocodile. [P]
> The giraffe is yellow and brown. [P] It's a yellow and brown giraffe. [P]
> The lion is orange. [P] It's an orange lion. [P]
> The monkey is purple. [P] It's a purple monkey. [P]

6 Give one of the pupils a bag containing two animals, two shapes and two fruits. Divide the class into groups. The pupils have to guess what is in the bag. The first group to get all six is the winner. The dialogue should resemble this:

Group 1	*Is there a monkey?*
Pupil	*No, there isn't.*
Group 2	*Is there a crocodile?*
Pupil	*Yes, there is.*
Group 3	*Is there a crocodile and a square?*
Pupil	*Yes, there is.*
Group 1	*Is there a crocodile, a square and a monkey?* etc.

7 If you are using the picture dictionary, pupils should turn to page 41 and write in the vocabulary (*elephant, lion, crocodile, monkey, snake, giraffe*).

Page 25 part 2

Active vocabulary
Can you see ...?

1 Play the dialogue and practise the use of *can*. Play the dialogues sentence by sentence for the pupils to repeat. Ensure that this use of *can* is understood.

[cassette] Can you see a monkey?
Yes, I can. [P]
Is it a green monkey?
No, it isn't. [P]
What colour is it?
It's purple. [P]

2 Build up further dialogues using the other animals. This should be done first with the whole class, then, if possible, in groups or pairs.

3 Play the complete version of the song 'Animals'. Let the pupils listen and then sing along with the cassette. If possible, while they are singing hold up a flashcard or picture of the appropriate animal as a prompt.

[cassette] The kangaroo is in the zoo. Let's go! Let's go!
The kangaroo is in the zoo. Let's go! Let's go!
The kangaroo is in the zoo
And the penguin's in there, too.
Let's all, let's all, let's all go to the zoo.

The elephant is in the zoo. Let's go! Let's go!
The elephant is in the zoo. Let's go! Let's go!
The elephant is in the zoo
And the monkey's in there, too.
Let's all, let's all, let's all go to the zoo.

The crocodile is in the zoo. Let's go! Let's go!
The crocodile is in the zoo. Let's go! Let's go!
The crocodile is in the zoo
And the lion is in there, too.
Let's all, let's all, let's all go to the zoo.

The tall giraffe is in the zoo. Let's go! Let's go!
The tall giraffe is in the zoo. Let's go! Let's go!
The tall giraffe is in the zoo
And the snake is in there, too.
Let's all, let's all, let's all go to the zoo.

[cassette] Look at the tall clown! [P] He's thin. [P]
Look at the short clown! [P] He's fat. [P]

Look at the princess! [P] She's beautiful. [P]
Look at the witch! [P] She's ugly. [P]

3 Colour dictation. Teach *blonde* before listening to the description of the princess.

[cassette] Look at the thin clown! [P] His trousers are red and white. [P] His jacket is blue. [P] His T-shirt is yellow and green. [P] His shoes are red. [P]
Look at the princess! [P] Her dress is pink and yellow. [P] Her hat is pink and yellow. [P] Her hair is blonde. [P] Her shoes are pink. [P]
Look at the fat clown! [P] His trousers are orange and blue. [P] His jacket is orange. [P] His hat is black. [P] His shoes are blue. [P]
Look at the witch! [P] Her dress is black and grey. [P] The stars and circles are yellow. [P] Her hat is black and yellow. [P] Her hair is black. [P]
Look at the ball! [P] It's red and blue. [P]
Look at the balloons! [P] The cat balloon is purple. [P] One balloon is green. [P]
Look at the triangle! [P] It's brown. [P] Look at the rectangle! [P] It's red. [P] Look at the square! [P] It's orange. [P]

4 The pupils listen to the descriptions of the witch. They should repeat each sentence.

[cassette] Look at the witch! [P] She's ugly. [P] Her hair is black. [P] Her dress is black and grey. [P] The circles and stars are yellow. [P] Her balloon is purple. [P]

With the class, build up descriptions of the other characters, for example *Look at the princess! She's beautiful. Her hair is blonde. Her dress is pink and yellow. Her hat is pink and yellow. Her shoes are pink.* Then select one or two more confident pupils and ask them to describe somebody either from the book or in the class. If time is available, more pupils could do this in groups.

Pages 26 – 7 part 1

Active vocabulary
witch princess fat thin beautiful ugly old new clown blonde

1 Teach *witch*, *princess*, and, *clown*. Revise *tall*, *short*, *big*, and *small*.

2 Using the cassette practise the new vocabulary and teach *thin*, *fat*, *beautiful*, and *ugly*.

Pages 26 – 7 part 2

Active vocabulary
in front of behind

1 Revise the prepositions, *on*, *in*, and *under*, using objects.

2 Teach the prepositions *in front of* and *behind*, using the cassette. To help consolidate them call

two pupils out to the front of the class. Stand one in front of the other and say *Look at Mary! She's in front of Sam. Look at Sam! He's behind Mary.* If necessary this can be practised in groups.

> 🔲 Look at the elephant! [P] It's big. [P]
> Look at the monkey! [P] It's on the elephant. [P]
> Look at the snake! [P] It's in the box. [P]
> Look at the tiger! [P] It's behind the seal. [P]
> Look at the seal! [P] It's in front of the tiger. [P]
> Look at the giraffe! [P] It's on the square box. [P]
> Look at the penguin! [P] It's on the triangle. [P]

3 Using classroom objects practise all the prepositions (*on, in, under, in front of,* and *behind.*) Toy animals and flashcards can also be used. With a confident class a competition could be organised with groups asking questions to other groups.

4 Colour dictation.

> 🔲 The monkey is pink. [P] It's a pink monkey. [P]
> The elephant is purple. [P] It's a purple elephant. [P]
> The seal is orange. [P] It's an orange seal. [P]
> The snake is yellow and green. [P] It's a yellow and green snake. [P]
> The giraffe is orange and brown. [P] It's an orange and brown giraffe. [P]
> The tiger is orange and black. [P] It's an orange and black tiger. [P]
> The penguin is black and white. [P] It's a black and white penguin. [P]
> The parrot is red, blue, and green. [P] It's a red, blue, and green parrot. [P]
> The ball in front of the snake is red and yellow. [P] It's a red and yellow ball. [P]
> The ball behind the tiger is blue and white. [P] It's a blue and white ball. [P]
> Look at the monkey! [P] His hat is grey and pink. [P] His balloon is blue. [P]

If time is available the pupils could colour in the rest of the page.

5 Listen to the questions and answers. The pupils should repeat both.

> 🔲 Where's the monkey? [P] It's on the elephant. [P]
> Where's the blue and white ball? [P] It's behind the tiger. [P]

Then ask more questions of the same type. For example *Where's the penguin? It's in front of the elephant. It's on the triangle. Where's the snake? It's in the box.*

6 Practise asking and answering similar questions, first with the whole class, then, if possible, in groups or pairs.

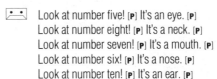

Page 28 part 1

Active vocabulary
mouth ear neck

1 Using the cassette and the pupils own faces, teach the new vocabulary. Revise *eye, hair,* and *nose.*

> 🔲 Look at number five! [P] It's an eye. [P]
> Look at number eight! [P] It's a neck. [P]
> Look at number seven! [P] It's a mouth. [P]
> Look at number six! [P] It's a nose. [P]
> Look at number ten! [P] It's an ear. [P]

Ask questions of the type *What's number five?*

2 Continue asking questions of this type. Then practise asking and answering questions first with the whole class, then, if possible, in groups or pairs.

3 Do the action rhyme 'Point to your mouth'. The pupils should cut out the pictures from page C2 and stick them in. Then they should join in and perform the actions.

> 🔲 Point to your mouth
> And touch your ears.
> Point to your eyes
> And touch your nose.
> Point to your neck
> And touch your toes.
>
> Point to your mouth
> And touch your ears.
> Point to your eyes
> And touch your nose.
> Point to your neck
> And touch your toes.

4 If you are using the picture dictionary, pupils should turn to page 41 and write in the vocabulary (*eyes, mouth, hair, neck, ears*).

Page 28 part 2

Active vocabulary
arm leg hand foot

1 Using the cassette and the pupils own bodies, teach the new vocabulary. Revise *eye* and *nose.*

[cassette] Look at number three! [P] It's a leg. [P]
Look at number four! [P] It's a foot. [P]
Look at number one! [P] It's an arm. [P]
Look at number two! [P] It's a hand. [P]

2 Ask questions of the type *What's number three?* Then practise asking and answering questions first with the whole class, then, if possible, in groups or pairs.

3 Do the action rhyme 'Touch your arm'. The pupils join in and perform the actions.

[cassette] Touch your arm
And touch your leg.
Touch your hand
And touch your foot.

Touch your arm
And touch your leg.
Touch your hand
And touch your foot.

4 Ask questions of the type *What colour are your eyes?* Then practise asking and answering questions first with the whole class, then, if possible, in groups or pairs.

5 If you are using the picture dictionary, pupils should turn to pages 41 and 42 and write in the vocabulary (*arm*, *hand*, *leg*, *foot*).

Page 29

Active vocabulary
address forty-six forty-seven forty-eight forty-nine fifty

1 The pupils listen to the two dialogues. They should repeat them sentence by sentence. Point out that the questions are prompted by the pictures on the page.

[cassette] A How old are you?
    B I'm eight. [P]
    A Are you a boy or a girl.
    B I'm a boy. [P]
    A What colour is your hair?
    B It's black. [P]
    A What colour are your eyes?

    B They're brown. [P]
    A What's your telephone number?
    B It's 54782. [P]
    A Where do you live?
    B In England. [P]

    A How old are you?
    B I'm seven. [P]
    A Are you a boy or a girl.
    B I'm a girl. [P]
    A What colour is your hair?
    B It's blonde. [P]
    A What colour are your eyes?
    B They're blue. [P]
    A What's your telephone number?
    B It's 675432. [P]
    A Where do you live?
    B In Scotland. [P]

2 Ask one or two pupils the same questions in front of the class. They should answer for themselves. When you feel that the pupils have understood the form of the dialogue the pupils can practise their own forms of the dialogue in pairs.

3 Listen to the cassette and teach the new numbers in the usual way.

[cassette] Forty-six, [P] forty-seven, [P] forty-eight, [P] forty-nine, [P] fifty. [P]

4 The pupils complete and colour the numbers the colours of their choice. Then working in pairs they should ask one another (and answer) questions like *What colour's forty-nine?*

5 Count from one to fifty (and if possible back again) around the class in a chain.

Page 30

Active vocabulary
What's the time? clock o'clock

1 If you have a teaching clock this should be used for the presentation of the time. If this is not available, draw twelve clock faces on the board, showing from one o'clock to twelve o'clock. As you say the time, point to the it on the teaching clock or the board and ask the pupils to repeat. For example *What's the time? It's one o'clock. What's the time? It's two o'clock.*

2 Using the teaching clock or the blackboard drawings, get the pupils to ask and answer the same questions.

3 The pupils open their books, listen to the cassette, and draw in the appropriate time on the appropriate clock.

> 🔲 Look at the cat clock. [P] What's the time?
> It's six o'clock. [P]
> Look at the dog clock. [P] What's the time?
> It's four o'clock. [P]
> Look at the snake clock. [P] What's the time?
> It's ten o'clock. [P]
> Look at the monkey clock. [P] What's the time?
> It's eight o'clock. [P]
> Look at the penguin clock. [P] What's the time?
> It's three o'clock. [P]
> Look at the crocodile clock. [P] What's the time?
> It's seven o'clock. [P]
> Look at the tiger clock. [P] What's the time?
> It's eleven o'clock. [P]
> Look at the lion clock. [P] What's the time?
> It's two o'clock. [P]
> Look at the elephant clock. [P] What's the time?
> It's twelve o'clock. [P]
> Look at the giraffe clock clock. [P] What's the time?
> It's one o'clock. [P]
> Look at the seal clock. [P] What's the time?
> It's five o'clock. [P]
> Look at the parrot clock. [P] What's the time?
> It's nine o'clock. [P]

When the clocks have all been completed, continue asking questions of this type, first with the whole class, then, if possible, in groups or pairs.

4 Play the song 'Tick-tock'. Let the pupils listen and then sing along with the cassette.

> 🔲 It's one o'clock, it's two o'clock, it's three o'clock.
> Tick-tock, tick-tock.
> It's four o'clock, it's five o'clock, it's six o'clock.
> Tick-tock, tick-tock.
> It's seven o'clock, it's eight o'clock, it's nine o'clock.
> Tick-tock, tick-tock.
> It's ten o'clock, it's eleven o'clock, it's twelve o'clock.
> Tick-tock, tick-tock, tick-tock.
> Tick-tock, tick-tock, tick-tock.
> Tick-tock, tick-tock, tick-tock, tick-tock.

5 The pupils choose (individually) any ten numbers between one and fifty. They write these in the squares at the bottom of the page. When they are ready, play 'Bingo'.

Page 31 part 1

Active vocabulary
cornflakes bread egg

1 Using the picture of Coco at the top of the page, teach *cornflakes*, *bread*, and *egg*.

2 Ask the question *Do you like …?* using the new vocabulary and also revising the food vocabulary already encountered (*apples*, *pears*, *ice-cream*, *biscuits*, *cake*, *bananas*, *lemons*, *strawberries*, *oranges*).

3 Ask the pupils *What's the time?* in relation to the picture. Revise the times learnt in the previous lesson.

4 If you are using the picture dictionary, pupils should turn to page 42 and write in the vocabulary (*bread* and *egg*).

Page 31 part 2

Active vocabulary
knife fork spoon sausages fish peas
tomato carrot mushrooms grapes cherries
honey

1 Using the cassette, and, if possible flashcards, teach the new vocabulary. The pupils should repeat the answers and answer for themselves where appropriate.

> 🔲 Look at number eight! [P] What is it? It's a fork. [P]
> Look at number six! [P] What is it? It's a spoon. [P]
> Look at number two! [P] What is it? It's a knife. [P]

Practise the new vocabulary, asking and answering questions as a whole class, then in pairs. Ask questions of the type *Number eight. What is it?*

2 Using the cassette, teach the new vocabulary.

> 🔲 Look at number fourteen! [P] What are they? They're sausages. [P]
> Look at number three! [P] What is it? It's a fish. [P]
> Look at number seven! [P] What is it? It's bread. [P]

Practise the new vocabulary, asking and answering questions as a whole class, then in pairs.

3 Listen to the dialogue. The pupils should listen, answer the questions, and then create similar dialogues in pairs, answering according to their own likes and dislikes.

> ▱ Candy   Coco, do you like sausages?
> Coco   Yes, I do. [P]
> Candy   Do you like fish?
> Coco   No, I don't. [P]

Ask questions directly to the pupils of the type *Do you like sausages?*

4   Teach the new vocabulary.

> ▱ Look at number eleven! [P] What is it? It's a carrot. [P]
> Look at number four! [P] What are they? They're mushrooms. [P]
> Look at number thirteen! [P] What are they? They're peas. [P]
> Look at number ten! [P] What is it? It's a tomato. [P]

Practise the new vocabulary, asking and answering questions as a whole class, then in pairs.

5   Listen to the dialogue. The pupils should listen, answer the questions, and then create similar dialogues in pairs, answering according to their own likes and dislikes.

> ▱ Candy   Coco, do you like carrots?
> Coco   Yes, I do. [P]
> Candy   Do you like mushrooms?
> Coco   No, I don't. [P]

Ask questions directly to the pupils of the type *Do you like carrots?*

6   Teach the new vocabulary.

> ▱ Look at number five! [P] What is it? It's honey. [P]
> Look at number one! [P] What is it? It's an egg. [P]
> Look at number nine! [P] What are they? They're grapes. [P]
> Look at number twelve! [P] What are they? They're cherries. [P]

Practise the new vocabulary, asking and answering questions as a whole class, then in pairs.

7   Listen to the dialogue. The pupils should listen, answer the questions, and then create similar dialogues in pairs, answering according to their own likes and dislikes.

> ▱ Candy   Coco, do you like honey?
> Coco   Yes, I do. [P]
> Candy   Do you like grapes?
> Coco   No, I don't. [P]

Ask more questions of the same type.

8   Play the song 'I like carrots'. Let the pupils listen and then sing along with the cassette. The pupils can point to another child as they sing *What do*

you like? With a confident class, pupils can substitute their own likes and sing their own verses, pointing to another pupil who will then continue.

> ▱ I like carrots, I like peas.
> I like carrots and peas.
> What do you like?
>
> I like mushrooms. I like grapes.
> I like mushrooms and grapes.
> What do you like?
>
> I like sausages. I like bread.
> I like sausages and bread.
> What do you like?
>
> I like tomatoes. I like fish.
> I like tomatoes and fish.
> What do you like?

9   If you are using the picture dictionary, pupils should turn to page 42 and write in the vocabulary (*Knife, fork, spoon, sausages, fish, peas, tomato, carrot, mushrooms, grapes, cherries, honey*).

Page 31 part 3

Active vocabulary
Can I help you?   Good morning   please   thank you   want

1   Listen to the dialogue in a shop. The pupils should repeat the new expressions. Ensure that these are understood.

> ▱ Shopkeeper   Good morning. Can I help you?
> Coco   Yes, please. I want three apples, four bananas and two oranges, please. [P]
> Shopkeeper   Here you are.
> Coco   Thank you. [P]

2   Pupils should practise the dialogue, substituting their own purchases. If possible, flashcards or real objects should be used to add realism. The dialogues can be acted out by two pupils in front of the class first and then in pairs.

3   Sing the song 'I like carrots'.

Page 32

Active vocabulary
sad happy tired poor rich

1 Using the cassette, teach the new vocabulary.

> 📼 Look at number one! [P] She's sad. [P]
> Look at number two! [P] He's happy. [P]
> Look at number three! [P] She's tired. [P]
> Look at number four! [P] He's poor. [P]
> Look at number five! [P] He's rich. [P]

2 Practise the answers *Yes, she is* and *Yes, he is*.

> 📼 Look at number one! [P] Is she sad?
> Yes, she is. [P]

Continue asking questions of the same type.

3 Practise the answers *No, she isn't* and *No, he isn't*

> 📼 Look at number one! [P] Is she happy?
> No, she isn't. She's sad. [P]

Continue asking questions of the same type.

4 Then, if possible move on to group or pair work practising both affirmative and negative answers.

5 Colour dictation.

> 📼 Look at the rich man. [P] His jacket is black. [P] His hat is grey. [P]
> Look at the poor man. [P] His jacket is red. [P] His T-shirt is green. [P] His hat is blue. [P]
> Look at the sad girl. [P] Her dress is red and blue. [P] Her hair is brown. [P] Her teddy bear is yellow. [P]
> Look at the tired girl. [P] Her skirt is pink. [P] Her sweater is pink and white. [P] Her hat is blue and red. [P]
> Look at the happy boy. His sweater is green.

Page 33

Active vocabulary
hungry thirsty hot cold young old

1 Using the cassette, teach the new vocabulary.

> 📼 Look at number six. [P] He's hungry. [P]
> Look at number seven. [P] She's thirsty. [P]
> Look at number eight. [P] She's hot. [P]
> Look at number nine. [P] She's cold. [P]
> Look at number ten. [P] He's young. [P]
> Look at number eleven. [P] He's old. [P]

2 Practise the new vocabulary, asking questions like *Number ten. What is it?*

3 Practise the tag answers, using pages 32 and 33. Ask questions like *Is number eight cold?*

4 Continue practising questions and answers of this type in groups or pairs.

5 Colour dictation.

> 📼 Look at the old man. [P] His jacket is blue. [P] His hat is green. [P]
> Look at the young boy. [P] His trousers are blue. [P] His sweater is yellow. [P]
> Look at the hungry boy. [P] His sweater is green. [P] His hair is brown. [P] His hat is blue and green. [P]
> Look at the thirsty girl. [P] Her sweater is purple. [P] Her hair is blonde. [P] Her eyes are blue. [P]
> Look at the hot girl. [P] Her dress is orange and green. [P] Her hair is brown. [P] The sun is yellow. [P]
> Look at the cold girl. [P] Her hat is green. [P] Her coat is blue and red. [P]

Page 34

Active vocabulary
ride a bicycle sing play tennis read draw

1 The pupils listen to the cassette. Ensure that they understand the new vocabulary. They should then answer the questions for themselves saying *Yes, I can* or *No, I can't*. You can check and revise the new vocabulary by saying, for example *Look at number three.* The pupils should answer *Read*.

> 📼 Look at number one! [P] Look at Coco! He can run. [P]
> Look at number two! [P] Look at Candy! She can walk. [P]
> Look at number three! [P] Look at Coco! He can read. [P]
> Look at number four! [P] Look at Candy! She can jump. [P]
>
> Can Coco run? Yes, he can. [P]
> Can Candy walk? Yes, she can. [P]

Continue asking questions of this type. Then ask questions directly to the pupils of the type *Can you read?* Continue as a class, or in groups, to practise similar questions and answers.

2 Listen to the rhyme 'I can walk'. Pupils should join in, and, if possible, perform the actions.

[cassette] I can walk, I can walk.
Can you walk? Can you walk?
Yes, I can. Yes I can.

I can run, I can run.
Can you run? Can you run?
Yes, I can. Yes I can.

I can read, I can read.
Can you read? Can you read?
Yes, I can. Yes I can.

3   The pupils listen to the cassette. Ensure that they understand the new vocabulary. They should then answer the questions for themselves saying *Yes, I can* or *No, I can't.*

[cassette] Look at number five! [P] Look at Coco! He can ride a bicycle. [P]
Look at number six! [P] Look at Candy! She can play tennis. [P]
Look at number seven! [P] Look at Coco! He can draw. [P]
Look at number eight! [P] Look at Candy! She can sing. [P]

Ask questions of the type *Can Coco ride a bicycle?* eliciting the answers *Yes, he can.* Then ask direct questions to the pupils of the type *Can you play tennis?* Continue as a class, or in groups, to practise similar questions and answers.

Page 35

Active vocabulary
fly tell dance cook swim play

1   The pupils listen to the cassette. Ensure that they understand the new vocabulary. They should then answer the questions for themselves saying *Yes, I can* or *No, I can't.* You can check and revise the vocabulary by saying *Look at number eleven!* The pupils should answer *Fly a kite.*

[cassette] Look at number nine! [P] Look at Coco! He can turn around. [P]
Look at number ten! [P] Look at Candy! She can touch her toes. [P]
Look at number eleven! [P] Look at Coco! He can fly a kite. [P]
Look at number twelve! [P] Look at Candy! She can dance. [P]

Ask questions as before to practice *Yes, he can* and *Yes, she can.* Then ask the questions directly

to the pupils *Can you ...* Continue as a class, or in groups, to practise similar questions and answers.

2   The pupils listen to the cassette. Ensure that they understand the new vocabulary. They should then answer the questions for themselves saying *Yes, I can* or *No, I can't.*

[cassette] Look at number thirteen! [P] Look at Coco! He can cook. [P]
Look at number fourteen! [P] Look at Candy! She can swim. [P]
Look at number fifteen! [P] Look at Coco! He can tell the time. [P]
Look at number sixteen! [P] Look at Candy! She can play ball. [P]

Ask questions as before. Continue as a class, or in groups, practising similar questions and answers.

3   Play the game 'Simon says' (see page 8) using as many of the action verbs as possible.

Page 36

Active vocabulary
What's missing?

1   The pupils look at picture one. Ask them *What can you see?* They should answer *I can see ...* You can also ask *Can you see a ...?* They should answer *Yes, I can* or *No, I can't.* Do the same with pictures three and five.

2   Ask the pupils to look at picture two and establish what is present in the same way. Then ask *What's missing?* and explain if necessary. The pupils should notice that the heart is missing in relation to picture one.

3   Do the same with pictures four and six in relation to pictures three and five.

4   The pupils should colour the pictures with colours of their own choice. They then ask one another questions about colours.